WILL YOU MARRY ME?

Proposals Famous and Infamous

EDITED BY HELENE SCHEU-RIESZ

Pictures by Helen Howell

ISLAND PRESS

COPYRIGHT, 1940, 1944,
BY HELENE SCHEU-RIESZ
ALL RIGHTS RESERVED

MANUFACTURED IN THE UNITED STATES OF AMERICA

In 1939 a Professor of a Creative Writing Department gave his class a proposal letter as an assignment. Discussion among the students revealed that the boys could not see any reason for writing such a letter. "I'd ring her up long distance," was the majority vote. One young man said: "I don't know much about girls, but if I was one and a fellow didn't know without writing a letter whether I wanted to marry him or not, I'd not care to have him as a husband."

The war has changed all that. Letter writing has again become part of life, and proposing by letter should become a wide-spread habit.

This volume is dedicated to the fighting forces at home and abroad—to the heroes who, while doing their duty as soldiers, are thinking of the other important capacity in which they will serve their country: providing for the future by founding a family.

George Edward Pickett's letters from camp are a fit ending to the war-time edition of this book.

Soldiers, sailors and pilots are invited to help gather, for the next printing, a rich crop of modern proposal letters, to boost the section classified as functional and modern.

New York, 1944

Helene Scheu-Riesz

Table of Contents

Introduction 1

Gothic 5

Renaissance 13

Baroque 31

Rococo 37

Directoire and Empire 43

The Victorians 67

The Moderns 99

Americana 109

Introduction

MARRIAGE IS BECOMING FASHIONABLE AGAIN, after an age of barnstorming revolutionists who looked for other ways of keeping the race going. It is taught at universities as a science; it is practiced in life and literature as an art. That is one of the reasons why a collection of proposal letters seems timely.

Many volumes of love letters have been published in English, but so far as I could discover, no proposal letters. The reasons are evident. Such letters are rare; people who write or receive them are seldom willing to exhibit them. Yet the few available are much more illuminating of personalities than any other documents they left. They show men and women at the crossroads of their lives; before the ultimate decision that will shape their own future and that of humanity in so far as they are part of it.

Love letters are as uniform as the passion that creates them. Proposals reflect social background; they picture society.

It has often been said that life copies art. Schools of painting have changed the faces and figures of men and women. Novels have created types of lovers. Churches, palaces and homes have influenced the development of people who lived around and in them. This shows in proposal letters; their style follows the style of architecture. The square heavy construction of the early Norman cathedral; the mystic upward swing of the slender Gothic arch; the clear classical stability of the Renaissance pillar; the round arches, turrets, vaults, bulging ornaments, and trumpeting angels of the Baroque; the fantastic grace and freakishness of the Rococo; the puritan simplicity, religious devotion and economic shrewdness of the early American colonists, the eclecticism, imitation and promiscuousness in styles of later colonists; the straightlined functionalism of the moderns—all can be traced in the proposal letters through the centuries. Cathedrals, fortresses, palaces, mansions, parliaments, log-cabins, cottages and apartment-houses rise behind them and form the background to the individual fate of famous men and women who asked the big question.

The pendulum of emotional expression swings between overstatement and understatement, romanticism and realism. Victorian prudery was followed by Edwardian license, and this again gives way to the spirit which prompts a king to give up his throne rather than be united to the woman he loves by a less binding ceremony than a church wedding.

Experts say that the history of evolution nearly always shows the male as the leader in the marriage game because he likes to hunt while the female prefers to be hunted. But if Hollywood pictures are a true reflection of contemporary life the game has been reversed. The majority show the hero as the hunted party. The heroine often needs a full evening's program to break his resistance. Is this the reality of a functional age or only dream and wish-fulfilment?

The polar explorer Sir Hubert Wilkins once told me how penguins propose.

When a male penguin meets a female attractive enough to make him think of marriage, he picks up a pebble from the ground and places it at her feet. She looks him over, and if she thinks he will do, she accepts the token and carries it to a secluded spot among the rocks where she would like to reside; and there and then the nest is built and family life started.

A Scott-Peary expedition to the South Pole had a painter along who used to sit sketching among the rocks. One morning a penguin came along and put a pebble down at his feet.

Sir Hubert did not say whether the painter accepted the token or just made a sketch of the wayward suitor.

According to the animal biographer Brehm, birds are the leaders in monogamy. They live in the only true marriage; they mate for life. Their proposals are recorded in music; and it is still the male who sings them.

4

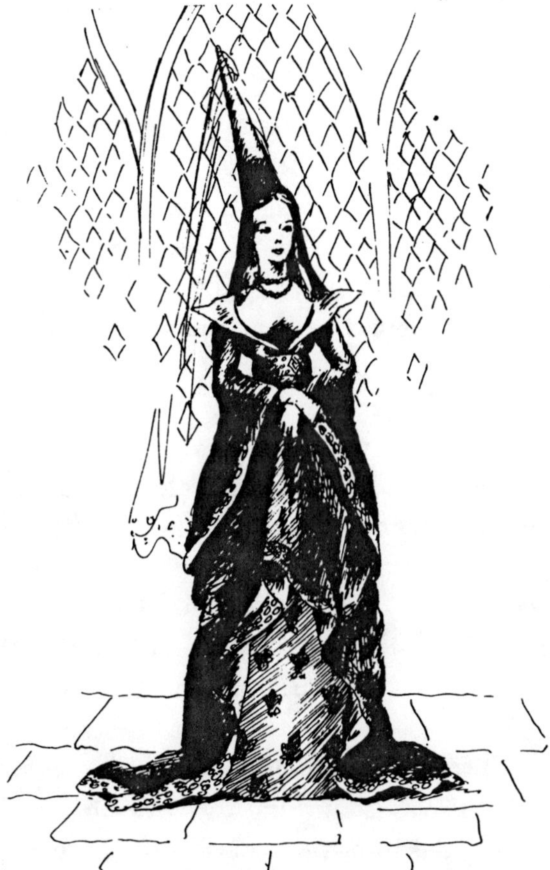

Gothic

LETTER-WRITING DID NOT BECOME a general practice before the discovery of America.

Not that the art of writing is new! The tombs of Egypt yield bronze pens of the best workmanship; but the Pharaohs have left no private correspondence. The parchments found in the pyramids are bills and accounts of household matters.

The earliest letter of proposal that can be traced was probably the epistle King David sent to his general Joab, when Bathsheba, the wife of Uriah, had taken the royal fancy. This grim proposal by proxy, dated 1035 B.C., runs:

"David to Joab, sent by the hand of Uriah the Hittite: Let ye Uriah in the forefront of the battle and retire ye from him that he may be smitten and die."

Seeing that such use was made of the technique of writing it is not astonishing that the Greeks, when it was introduced into their country about that time, looked upon it as something evil—the way alchemy and astrology were looked upon later in history. Many of the early letters pertaining to royal marriages bear out the sinister meaning of the word "runic." Archives of the courts still reveal cartloads of information illuminating the dark ages when kingdoms could only be acquired by war or marriage—equally cruel—and when it was customary to get rid of enemies, wives or husbands, by poison.

One of these letters, though not a proposal in the strict sense, throws so much light upon the way marriages were proposed and settled at the time that it seems to belong here to paint the background.

Isabella of Angoulême, as a young child, had been engaged to Hugh de Lusignan, a Norman nobleman, and given into his custody. When she was twelve, King John of England demanded her hand in marriage, and her father, preferring a king as a son-in-law, took her away from Lusignan. To appease his fury, the first daughter of John and Isabella was, from the cradle, engaged to him.

King John was not easy to live with. Far from faithful himself, he was jealous and had a habit of hanging his wife's admirers at the head of her bed. When he died—poisoned by a monk for trying to rape the abbot's sister—Isabella quickly robbed her infant daughter of her fiancé and married him herself. Her letter to her young son Henry III neatly explains how she did it all in pure, unselfish, motherly devotion:

Royal Letter No. 592, Tower of London Anno Domini 1220

Isabella of Angoulême, Queen Dowager and Countess of March and Angoulême, to King Henry of England

We hereby signify to you that when the Earls of March and Eu departed this life, the Lord Hugh de Lusignan remained alone and without heirs in Poictou, and his friends would not permit that our daughter should be united to him by marriage, because her age is so tender; but counselled him to take a wife from whom he might speedily hope for an heir; and it was proposed that he should take a wife in France, which if he had done, all your land in Poictou and Gascony should be lost. We therefore, seeing the great peril that might accrue to you if that marriage took place, married the said Hugh Earl of March ourselves; and God knows that we rather did it for your benefit than our own. Wherefore we entreat you, as our dear son, that this thing may be pleasing to you, seeing that it conduces greatly to the profit of you and yours; and we earnestly pray that you restore to him his lawful right, that is Niort, the castles of Exeter and Rockingham and 3500 marks which your father, our former husband, bequeathed to us; and so, if it please you, deal with him who is so powerful, that he may not remain against you, since he can serve you well . . . and if it shall please you, you may send for our daughter, your sister, by a trusty messenger and letters patent, and we will send her to you.

Isabella was beautiful and mischievous. She did not send her daughter, but kept her as a sort of hostage, to put pressure on the king, her son. She intrigued against him and put all sorts of difficulties in his way.

The plight in which Margery Brews, who later became Mrs. John Paston, found herself when she wrote the following letter, is an example of what marriages mostly were concerned with in the fifteenth century, among wealthy commoners as among royalty.

Unto my right well-beloved Valentine, John Paston Esqu. be this bill delivered: 1477

Right reverend and worshipful and right-beloved Valentine, I recommend me to you full heartily, desiring to hear of your welfare, which I beseech the Almighty God long for to preserve . . . And if it please you to hear of my welfare, I am not in good hele of body nor heart nor shall be till I hear from you.

And my lady my mother hath belabored the matter to my father full diligently, but she can no more get than ye know of; for which God knoweth I am full sorry. But if ye love me as I trust verily that ye do, ye will not leave me therefore. For if ye had not half the livelihood that ye have for to do the greatest labor that any woman alive might I would not forsake you.

No more to you at this time, but the Holy Trinity have you in keeping. And I beseech you that this bill be not seen by none earthly creature save yourself.

And this letter was indited at Topcroft, with full heavy heart

by your own
MARGERY BREWS

Arthur, Prince of Wales, eldest son of Henry VII, was engaged to the Spanish princess, Catharine of Aragon. Her parents, Ferdinand and Isabella, postponed the marriage for two years, till the bridegroom had completed his fourteenth year and the bride was fifteen.

They were married in November, 1501, and five months later Catharine was a widow. Henry VII was so afraid that he would have to pay back Catharine's dowry and would lose the alliance with Spain that he urged the engagement of his second son Henry to the young widow. That the boy was only eleven at the time and Catharine seventeen when this plan was evolved, did not hinder the father and Catharine's friends both in England and in Spain from campaigning for a speedy celebration of the marriage. Special permission had to be obtained from the Pope, who was glad to give it because he hoped the union would strengthen the Roman Church in England. Young Henry resisted for awhile and registered doubts about the validity of such a marriage but he married Catharine in the end.

Arthur, Prince of Wales, to Catharine of Aragon 1499

Most illustrious and excellent lady, my dearest spouse,

I wish you very much health . . . I have read the sweet letters of your Highness, from which I have easily perceived your entire love for me. Truly your letters traced by your own hand have so delighted me and have rendered me so cheerful and jocund that I fancied I beheld your Highness and conversed with and beheld my dearest wife. I cannot tell you what an earnest desire I feel to see your Highness, and how vexatious is to me this procrastination of your coming . . . let it be hastened that instead of absent we may be present with each other, and the loves conceived between us may reap their proper fruit . . .

From our castle of Ludlow, 5th of October 1499

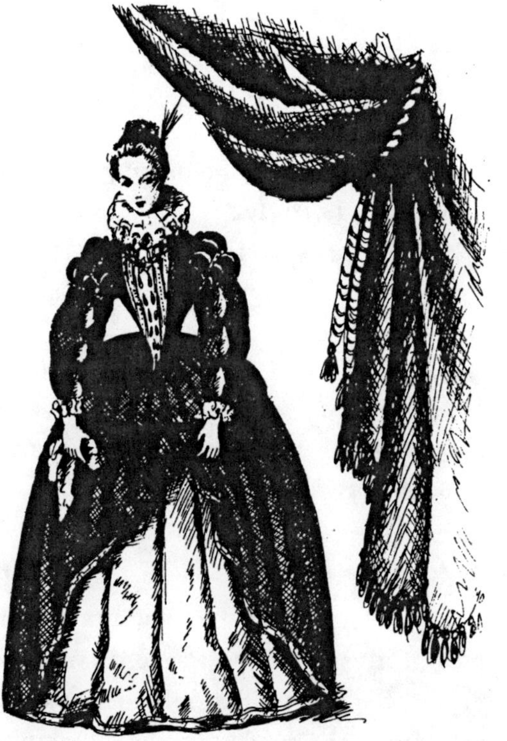

Renaissance

Henry VIII was the first English king raised in the ideas of the Renaissance. Had Catharine given him the son he craved, the schism which brought about the founding of the Church of England might never have occurred. As it was, Henry broke away from Catharine and the Pope at the same time. The next letter shows how he wooed Anne Boleyn, the second lady on his long marriage list.

Henry married Anne in 1533 and had her beheaded in 1536. Only a few months after having made her his queen, he was writing letters of the same kind to her successor, Jane Seymour.

Henry VIII to Anne Boleyn   *Undated*

By revolving in my mind the contents of your last letters I have put myself into great agony, not knowing how to interpret them, whether to my disadvantage (as I understood some others) or not. I beseech you earnestly to let me know your real mind as to the love between us two. It is needful for me to obtain this answer from you, having been for a whole year wounded with the dart of love and not yet assured whether I shall succeed in finding a place in your heart and affections. This uncertainty has hindered me of late from declaring you my mistress . . . lest it should prove that you only entertain an ordinary regard for me. But if you please to do the duty of a true and loyal mistress and to give yourself heart and person to me, who will be, as I have been, your most loyal servant (if your rigor does not forbid me) I promise you that not only the name shall be given you but also that I will take you for my mistress, cutting off all others that are in competition with you, out of my thoughts and affections, and serving you only. I beg you to give an entire answer to this my rude letter, that I may know on what and how far I may depend; but if it does not please you to answer me in writing, let me know some place where I may have it by word of mouth, and I will go thither with all my heart.

No more for fear of tiring you. Written by the hand of him who will willingly remain

Your

HENRY REX

As described by a contemporary, Jane Seymour was not striking. Of middle height and pallid complexion, she was not considered beautiful. "She is twenty-five," Chapuys says of her, "and you may imagine whether she, being an Englishwoman and having been so long at court, would not hold it a sin to be still a maid. At which the king will be rather pleased . . . for he will marry her on condition she is a virgin and when he wants a divorce he will find plenty of witnesses to the contrary."

But Jane, contrary to these expectations, escaped the fate of Catherine and Anne. More than any of his wives Henry loved Jane and mourned her when she died in childbirth—giving him the son he craved.

Henry VIII to Jane Seymour   1536

My dear friend and Mistress,

The bearer of these few lines from thy entirely devoted servant will deliver into thy fair hands a token of my true affection for thee, hoping you will keep it forever in your sincere love for me. Advertising you that there is a ballad made lately of great derision against us, which if it go much abroad and is seen by you, I pray you to pay no manner of regard to it. I am not at present informed who is the setter forth of this malignant writing, but if he is found out he shall be straitly punished for it. For the things ye lacked, I

have minded my Lord to supply them to you as soon as he can buy them. Thus hoping shortly to receive you in these arms, I am for the present
        Your own loving servant and sovereign
                         HENRY REX

Mary Tudor, younger sister of Henry VIII, as a child of eleven was engaged to Charles of Castille who later became the great Emperor Charles V. He addressed her in several letters as his wife, but the marriage never took place; it was prevented by some of his friends. Many years later, visiting the court of Henry VIII, Charles saw Mary as the wife of the Duke of Suffolk; he was so moved by her beauty that he, bitterly regretting her loss, refused to dance at the court ball given in his honor and sat apart, silent and moody, for the whole evening.

Early in 1514 Henry negotiated a political marriage between his lovely sister and Louis XII, of France, who was then old, sick and decrepit, but had become violently enamoured with a portrait of Mary. She at that time was in love with one of her brother's favorite courtiers, Charles Brandon, Duke of Suffolk. To induce her to marry Louis, Henry promised her that she should on the old king's death (which couldn't be far off) be allowed to marry Brandon, who, moreover, would be sent to France as British Ambassador.

Mary Tudor to King Louis of France

Humbly and with good grace I recommend me. Because the King, my lord and brother, presently sends his Ambassador to you I have desired, ordered and charged my cousin, the Earl of Worcester, to tell you some things from me touching the espousals now bespoken between you and me. So I beseech you, my lord, as I have before written and signified to you by my cousin, the Duke of Longueville, that the thing which I most desire and wish is to hear good news of your health and good prosperity, as my cousin, the Earl of Worcester, will tell you more fully. It will please you, moreover, my lord, to use and command me according to your good and agreeable pleasure, that I may obey and please you, by the help of God; who give you, my lord, good and long life.

By the hand of your humble companion
MARY

Her entrance into France was a triumph. Her beauty, dignity and royal grace won her the hearts. She was a good queen. But Henry did not keep his promise to send Brandon, or had not the authority to keep him at her court. Jealous old Louis isolated his beautiful bride from all her friends from home, even her women attendants.

When King Louis died Mary wanted to marry Brandon. But it looked as if she might become once more a pawn on the political chessboard. The new king, Francis I. though married to Louis' daughter and calling Mary "mother", was madly in love with her and pursued her with dishonorable addresses. She sought help from her brother.

Mary Tudor to King Henry VIII.

Pleaseth it your grace, the French king on Tuesday last night came to visit me and had with me many diverse discoursing, among the which he demanded me whether I had ever made any promise of marriage in any place, assuring me upon his honor and upon the word of a prince that in case I would be plain with him in that affair, that he would do for me therein to the best of his power, whether it were in his realm or out of the same. Whereunto I answered that I would disclose unto him the secret of my heart in humility, as to the prince of the world in whom, after your grace, I had the most trust, and so I declared unto him the good mind which for diverse considerations I bear to my lord Suffolk asking him not only to grant me his favor and consent thereunto, but also that he would of his own hand write unto Your Grace, and pray you to bear your like favor unto me and be content with the same; the which he granted me to do. And, Sire, I most humbly beseech you to take this answer which I made to the French king in good part, the which I only did to be discharged of the extreme pain and annoyance I was in by reason of such suit as the French king made unto me not according to my honour.

I most humbly beseech your grace to consider, in case that you make difficulty to condescend to the promises as I wish, the French king will take new courage to renew his suits to me; assuring you that

I had rather be out of the world than it should so happen; and how he shall entreat my lord of Suffolk, God knoweth, with many other inconveniences, which might ensue of the same, the which I pray our Lord that I may never have life to see.

By your loving sister and true servant,
MARY QUEEN OF FRANCE.

When this letter brought no results, Mary decided to take her fate into her own hands. She persuaded Brandon to marry her without anybody's consent. That was not quite easy, for he had given King Henry his promise not to do anything of the kind. The following letter to Henry is his report of the interview in which Mary broke his resistance.

Charles Brandon, Duke of Suffolk, to King Henry VIII
Sire,
When I came to Paris the Queen was in hand with me the first day, and said she must be short with me and show me her pleasure and mind, and so she began unto me and show how good lady she was to me, and if I would be ordered by her she would never have none but me, and she showed me she had verily understood as well by friar Langley and friar F . . tar that an ever she came into England she should never have me nor never come to England. And when I heard her say so I showed her that she said that but to prove me with, and she said that I

would not you know well; that at my coming to Paris how it was showed her, and I asked her what that was, and she said that the best in France had been unto her, that an she went into England she should go to Flanders, to which she said she had rather to be torn in pieces than ever she would come there, and with that weeped. I never saw woman so weep. And when I saw that I showed her grace that there was none such thing, by my faith with the best words I could, but in no wise could make her believe it; and when I saw that I showed her grace, an her grace would be content to write unto your grace and obtain your good will, I would be content, or else I durst not, because I made your grace such a promise; whereunto in conclusion she said: "If the King my brother is content, and the French king, both the one by his letters and the other by his words, that I should have you, I will have the time after my desire, or else I may well think that the words of them in these parts and of them in England are true; and that is that you are come to tice me hence to the intent that I may be married into Flanders, the which I will never to die for it, and so I promised the French king ere you came; and thus if so be you will not be content to follow after my mind, look, never after this day shall you have the proffer again. And, sire, I saw me in that case, and I thought . . . but rather to put me into your mercy than to lose all, and so I granted thereunto, and so she and I was married.

The following letter is a more formal document in which the king and his council was informed of the secret love-match and the queen takes all the blame in order to shield her husband. The date of this letter must have been early April 1515, for on April 16 Mary and Brandon left Paris, received full pardon on their arrival in England and were solemnly remarried in Greenwich, on May 13th.

My most dear and entirely beloved brother,

In most humble manner I recommend me to your grace. Dearest brother, I doubt not but that you have in your good remembrance that whereas for the good of peace and for the furtherance of your affairs you moved me to marry with my lord and late husband, king Louis of France, whose soul God pardon. Though I understood that he was very old and sickly, yet for the advancement of the said peace, and for the furtherance of your causes, I was contented to conform myself to your said motion, so that if I should fortune to survive the said late king I might with your good will marry myself at my liberty without your displeasure. Whereunto, good brother, you condescended and granted, as you well know, promising unto me that in such case you would never provoke or move me but as mine own heart and mind should be best pleased; and that wheresoever I should dispose myself, you would wholly be contented with the same. And upon that, your good comfort and faithful promise, I assented to the said marriage, which else I would never have granted to, as at the same time shewed unto you more at large.

Now that God has called my said late husband to his mercy, and that I am at my liberty, dearest brother, remembering the great virtues which I have seen and perceived heretofore in my lord Suffolk, to whom I have always been of good mind, as you well know, I have affixed and clearly determined myself to marry with him; and the same I assure you hath proceeded only of my own mind, without any request or labor of my said lord Suffolk, or of any other person. And to be plain with your grace, I have so bound myself unto him that for no cause earthly I will or may vary or change from the same. Wherefore my good and most kind brother, I now beseech your grace to give unto me and to my said lord Suffolk your good will therein . . . And to the intent it may please you the rather to condescend to this my most hearty desire, I am contented and expressly bind myself unto you, by these presents, to give you all the whole dote (dowry) which was delivered with me, and also all such plate of gold and jewels as I shall have of my late husband's. Over and besides this . . . I shall give you as much yearly part of my dower, to as great a sum as shall stand with your will and pleasure . . .

Either Henry was won over by the promise of dowry, plate and silver, or he was touched by an emotion expressed in his sister's letters that was echoed in his own heart; anyway, the couple obtained his forgiveness and was received and officially married in England.

Mary of France, young, beautiful, spirited and courageous, showed even in those dark ages when women had no voice in public affairs, that she could get the man she wanted. She refused to bear a son to an unloved king and married according to the dictation of her own heart.

The feminists ought to canonize her.

Realism had won the fight against mysticism when Anne Boleyn's daughter Elizabeth ascended the throne. Young, charming, queen of a rich and powerful realm, she was the most attractive prize on the marriage market where alliances decided the fate of nations. But she was averse to marriage, or appeared to be so.

Immediately after the death of her father, the Admiral of the Fleet, one of Jane Seymour's brothers, asked for her hand. She refused him and he consoled himself with her father's widow, Catharine Parr. This early experience must have left her somewhat cynical, and she did not take the later proposals of royal suitors very seriously. The next to be turned down was her brother-in-law, Philip II of Spain. After him the Austrian Hapsburgs entered the lists. Their archives were recently opened in Vienna and revealed the most amazing reports of the envoys to England who for half a decade peddled the Illustrious Archduke Charles to Elizabeth, with no success. She insisted that he should come to England to be inspected; they declared inspection impossible because if he came and was refused it would mean a slight which the Illustrious Archduke could not accept. While the argument over this question of etiquette went on, the envoys wrote reports of enquiries concerning the "maiden honor and integrity" of the Queen, finding that "all the aspersions against her are but spawn of envy, malice and hatred" and that the Earl of Leicester, her Master of the Horse, was a "virtuous, pious, courteous and highly moral man whom the Queen loves as a brother, in most chaste and honest love." In a special message the envoy implores the Archduke to dress well and not to ride on hacks but to use the finest palfreys because he had no doubt the Queen would send secret inspectors to see whether he was as handsome as described. After eight years of such diplomatic courtship the persistent wooer sends this letter of proposal.

Archduke Charles of Austria to Queen Elizabeth of England   Vienna, October 8, 1567

Illustrious Queen and Lady, Beloved and Venerated Cousin, Greeting, All Happiness, and the Assurance of My Sincere and Unfailing Willingness to serve you.

The Noble Earl of Sussex has delivered to us the much coveted letter from Your Highness, and then, as commanded orally and with much eloquence set forth all that your Highness in your sincerity, affection and kindness, intended for us. This afforded us much pleasure and solace. And though prior to this we had always been devoted to your Highness and studious of all that would be acceptable to you, this magnanimous and splendid proof of your good-will has endeared you still more to us; and we candidly avow that we shall also in future endeavor to preserve for ourself this benevolence and to foster its growth; for we know nothing more agreeable and desirable than to adore your Highness with worthy thoughts, honors and eulogies. . . .

As regards the negotiations themselves, which the noble Earl of Sussex is now conducting with His Imperial Majesty our liege-lord and brother in our affairs, we would not pester your Highness with verbose recapitulations, more especially as we do not doubt that the Earl will accomplish everything in entire concordance with Your Highness' wishes.

May it please your Highness, however, to learn from these lines that insofar as it is compatible with our conscientious belief, we shall in this present business endeavor to accommodate ourself to Your Highness' wishes, and besides in this as in all other matters be studious of your desires.

We are convinced that Your Highness as Queen and Princess, endowed with clemency and courtesy and distinguished with every kind of virtue, will with the same special affection, answer us in kindness and good-will, and will be at all pains to comprehend, that we shall in all sincerity use our best endeavors to gratify your Highness, and to demonstrate our zeal by deeds, if Eternal and Merciful Heaven preserve us in health and strength and bless our undertakings with success.

We commend ourself to Your Highness as
Your most devoted cousin
CHARLES, *Arch-Duke of Austria*

Christina, Queen of Sweden, daughter of the beloved king Gustaf Adolf, brilliant, neurotic, learned and strongwilled royal tom-boy, wrote the following letter when she was eighteen; she was crowned when nineteen and terminated the Thirty Years War when twenty-two—making peace against the passionate opposition of her chancellor Oxenstjerna and of her whole militaristic cabinet.

Her cousin Karl Adolf, more of a soldier than a lover, described as "ugly, dumpy, thick-set, common", could not retain her affection. In the end, rather than marry him she handed him the crown of Sweden and ran off to Rome where she lived and died as an adventurous exile.

Queen Christina of Sweden to Prince Karl Gustaf

January 5, 1644

Beloved Cousin,

I see by your letter that you do not trust your thoughts to the pen. We may, however, correspond with all freedom, if you send me the key to a cipher, and compose your letters according to it, and change the seals, as I do with mine. Then the letters may be sent to your sister, the Princess Maria. You must take every precaution, for never were people here so much against us as now; but they shall never get their way, so long as you remain firm. They talk a great deal of the Elector of Brandenburg, but neither he nor any one in the world, however rich he be, shall ever alienate my heart from you. My love is so strong that it can only be overcome by death, and if, which God forbid, you should die before me, my heart shall remain dead for every other, and my mind and affection shall follow you to eternity, there to dwell with you.

Perhaps some will advise you to demand my hand openly; but I beseech you, by all that is holy, to have patience for some time, until you have acquired some reputation in the war, and until I have the crown on my head. I entreat you not to consider this time long, but to think of the old saying: "He does not wait too long who waits for something good." I hope, by God's blessing, that it is a good thing we both are waiting for.

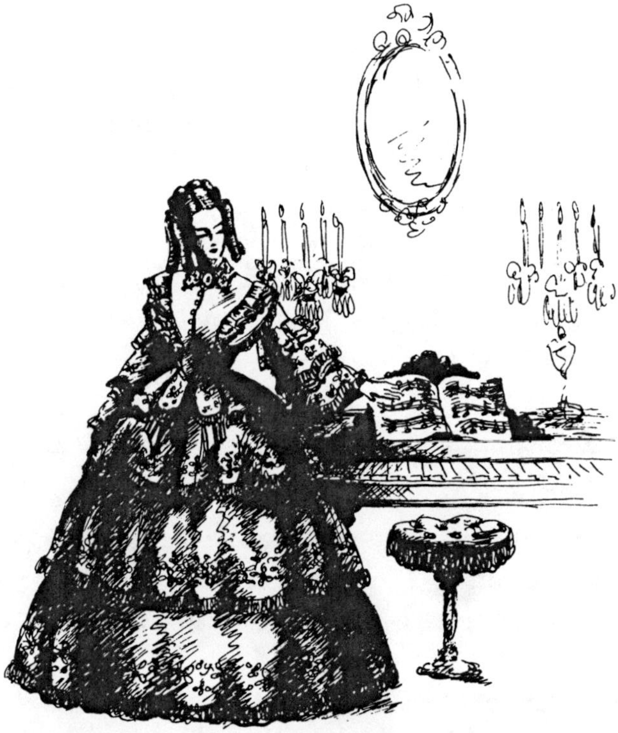

Baroque

Oliver Cromwell's youngest daughter, Frances, independent, modern-thinking, highly intelligent, brilliant, married, against her father's wishes, a grandson of the Earl of Warwick, who left her a widow after five weeks. John Russell courted her in many letters, which she parried with all the smooth technique of an experienced heart-breaker. She surrendered in the end to become his wife.

John Russell to Lady Frances Rich, daughter of Oliver Cromwell   1662 (?)

Love and fear, grief and impatience, are my perpetual tormentors. I cannot sleep but with a great deal of disturbance, I have not the same advantage of air as other men, I do not so much breathe as sigh. This is the condition I have been in ever since I saw you last, and now, Madam, that I have made known my torments to you, give me leave to tell you that there is nothing in this world can give me anything of ease but one line from your Ladyship, for which I as earnestly beg as I would for a morsel of bread if I were ready to starve; and since, Madam, it is in your power to take me off this rack, it concerns your generosity very much not to use cruelty to one who cries you quarter, and casts himself at your feet, where I beg that you would be pleased sometime that I am, Madam, your Ladyship's most humble and dutiful servant.

J. R.

Thomas Otway dedicated all the principal parts in his plays to Madame Barry, the actress. She kept him in suspense for seven years. He died without winning her.

This letter was written at the time of the brilliant success of Otway's "Venice Preserved," which made him one of the first dramatists and her the first actress of their age.

Thomas Otway, playwright, to Madame Barry, actress.   *1682*

Could I see you without passion or be absent from you without pain, I need not beg your pardon for thus renewing my vows that I love you more than health, or any happiness here or hereafter. Everything you do is a new charm to me, and though I have languished for seven long years of desire, jealously despairing, yet every minute I see you I still discover something new and more bewitching. Consider how I love you; what would I not renounce and enterprize for you? I have you mine or I am miserable, and nothing but knowing which shall be the happy hour can make the rest of my years that are to come, tolerable. . . .

Remember poor OTWAY

John Hervey published the seventy letters which his father, Thomas Hervey, and his mother exchanged before they married. These were Attic in style. He himself, after the death of his first wife, fell in love with Elizabeth Felton, and after settling financial matters with her father, wrote to her in true Baroque.

John Hervey to Elizabeth Felton   July 20, 1695
My ever-new Delight

    The grateful goodness you have shown in bringing so much nicety of taste and natural indifference as you are owner of to sett some little value upon a man whose greatest meritt is loving and thinking of you as he does, abates of the vanity might otherwise have been justly charg'd upon me in supposing that you should interess your self enough in what concerns me to care how I passd my journey; but the kind permission you allow'd me to take the pleasing liberty of writing to you being a further warrant and excuse for the trouble I am giving you, I will employ the happy priviledg to better purpose than acquainting you with my being well come to this place. Lett me bestow it in venting and doing justice to a heart full of love & faithfulness towards you. To tell you it is everything you coud wish it in your regard is not yet expressing rightly what it means and feels for you; no, saying it pays you by anticipation all that you can invent or expect or require from it, (were your demands unreasonable enough to be proportioned to the virtues which lay claim to it) would not come up to that degree of love and admiration Armida's charming prettynesses and touching decencies have created in it.

> Thou'rt now become my thoughts perpetual theme,
> Their daily longing and their nightly dream.

To please and make thee happy shall be the sole drift & constant meditation of my soul; and whenever I steal a moment's consideration that doth not tend directly and immediately to that end, 'tis how to make myself so in thee; in order whereunto I have been this night with Mr. Folkes, who hath promised to give the most expeditious turn to my affair that his witt can contrive; but saies it is not practicable by Tuesday; had it been so, my impatience to see thee again is such that even that day, so early as he may count it, would have been and is look'd upon as distant as doomsday to an expectation like mine. And now I have said this, lett me ask your pardon for the rest I broke you of the night before I died; (for is it not a death when soul and body separate?) But now I think on't, if that be a fault, no body is so criminal as yourself toward me; lett us then cry Quitts as to that matter; but I must observe, you could sleep when I was there present, which is more than he can do absent, who is, sleeping or waking, dead or living, worthy Armida's unworthy lover, friend and servant

J. H.

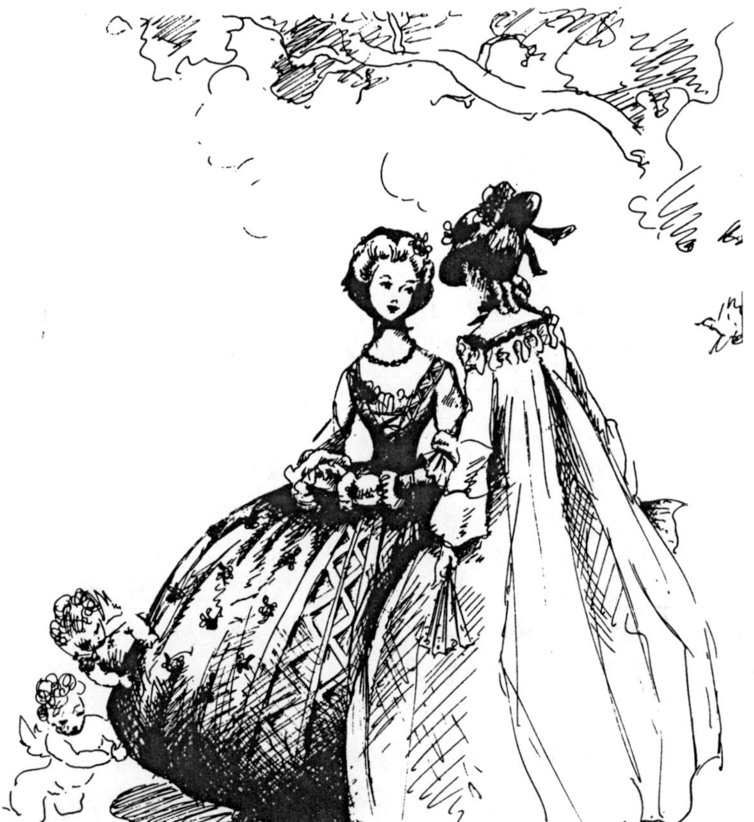

Rococo

Richard Steele, later co-editor of the Tatler *and the* Spectator, *left Cambridge University without a degree, to join the army. An impecunious but attractive captain, in 1705 he married a wealthy elderly widow, Mrs. Stretch, who died a year later. On the occasion of her funeral, he met Miss Mary Scurlock. In 1707 he married her secretly, perhaps to escape the charge of being too quickly consoled in his bereavement. "Dear Prue" tried to keep him out of debt but did not always succeed. She was genuinely attached to him and preserved all his letters, over four hundred. In them he calls her, before the wedding, his "charmer and inspirer"; afterwards, his "ruler and his absolute governess."*

Richard Steel to Mary Scurlock

Ld. Sunderland's Office. 1707

Madam,

With what language shall I address my lovely fair, to acquaint her with the sentiments of an heart she delights to torture? I have not a minute's quiet out of your sight; and when I'm with you, you use me with so much distance that I am still in a state of absence, heightened with a view of the charms I am denied to approach. In a word, you must give me either a fan, a mask or a glove you have worn, or I cannot live; otherwise you must expect I'll kiss your hand, or, when I next sit by you, steal your handkerchief. You yourself are too great a bounty to be received at once; therefore I must be prepared by degree, lest the might gift distract me with joy. Dear Mrs. Scurlock, I am tir'd with calling you by that name; therefore say the day in which you will take that of, Madam,

 your most obedient, most devoted humble servant
RICHARD STEELE

One of the great ironists of the eighteenth century, Jonathan Swift, whose savage satire, "Gulliver's Travels," became, ironically, a juvenile best-seller, had two abortive romances. Some biographers insist that he was secretly married to Esther Johnson, the "Stella" of his poems, though it is certain that Swift never lived with Stella. Another young girl, "Vanessa," spent her life yearning for Dean Swift's love, but when she found he would not marry her, she died of a broken heart—and consumption.

This next letter is one of mock proposal, addressed to a married woman, Mrs. Howard, Lady of the Bedchamber to Queen Caroline. It refers to the severe headaches from which she suffered.

Jonathan Swift to Mrs. Howard, Lady of the Bedchamber to Queen Caroline

Twickenham, August 14, 1727

Madam,

I wish I were a young lord and you were unmarried. I should make you the best husband in the world; for I am ten times deafer than you ever were in your life, and instead of a poor pain in the face I have good substantial giddiness and head-ache. The best of it is that though we might lay our heads together, you could tell me no secrets that might not be heard five rooms distant. These disorders of mine, if they hold as long as they used to do some years ago, will last as long as my license of absence—which I shall not renew, and then the Queen will have the misfortune not to see me, and I shall go back with the satisfaction never to have seen her since she was queen, but when I kissed her hands; and although she were a thousand queens, I will not lose my privilege of never seeing her but when she commands it.

I told my two landlords here that I would write you a love-letter, which I remembered you commanded me to do last year; but I would not show it to either of them. I am the greatest courtier and flatterer you have; because I try your good sense and taste more than all of them put together, which is the greatest compliment I could put upon you, and you have hitherto behaved yourself tolerably under it . . . I will say another thing in your praise—that goodness would become you better than any other person I know, and for that very reason there is nobody I wish to be good as much as yourself.

I am, ever, with the truest respect and esteem & &
JONATHAN SWIFT

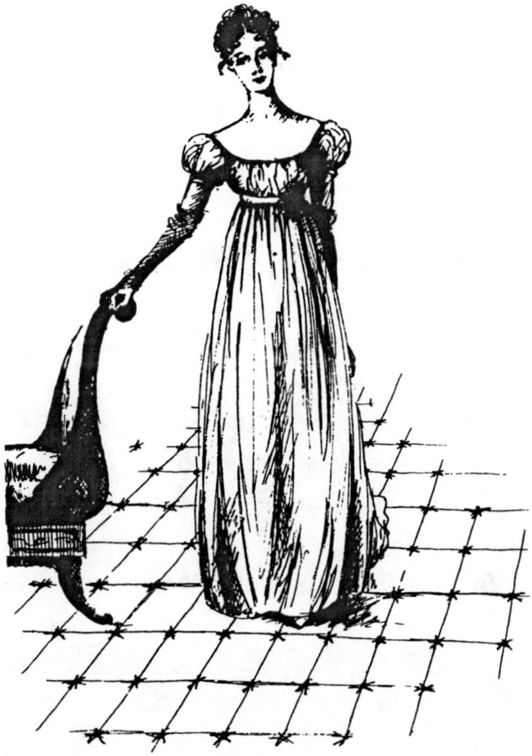

Directoire and Empire

The eighteenth century produced a male fore-runner of Emily Post. He was fifty years old, a printer in a publishing firm. His employer suggested that he should write a manual of letters for "important family occasions", something in the line of the messages which Western Union now offers to its clients. The manual was a success and the writer, incidentally, became the father of the modern English novel. His name was Samuel Richardson.

Everybody wrote letters now. The universal fashion rubbed off some of the individual charm of the earlier documents. In exchange for it there came a general fluency of language which sometimes grew into formality and ended up in the rigid stiffness, coldness and severity of the "Empire". The Empire style had its source in Napoleon's desire to revive the grandeur of the old Roman Empire. Its best presentation is Napoleon's own proposal letter to the Archduchess Maria Louisa of Austria.

"L'Empire" was eclectic in its combination of Renaissance, Byzantine and Egyptian elements. Its metallic ornaments symbolize military rule of minds and bodies. It led up to the mixture of all possible and impossible styles characteristic of the Victorian age.

FROM SAMUEL RICHARDSON'S "FAMILIAR LETTERS ON IMPORTANT OCCASIONS"

Hodge the Plowman to his Sweetheart Joan   *1739*

Sweet Honey Joan,

I have sent thee a thing, such a one as the Gentlefolk call a love letter, it was indited by myself after I had drunk two or three pots of ale, but it was written in Roman joining hand by the schoolmaster who is clark of the parish, to whom I gave sixpence for his pains. Truly Joan, and Marry Joan, thou knowest how many a time and oft I have fetched home the cows when nobody knew who did it. Marry Joan, thou knowest I always played on thy side at Stool-Ball; and when thou didst turn the garland in the Whitsun holidays, I was sure to be drunk that night with joy. Marry Joan, cry I still, but wilt thou marry me, Joan? I know thou doest love Will the Taylor, who, it is true, is a very quiet man and foots it most fetuously; but I can tell thee, Joan, I think I shall be a better man than he very shortly, for I am learning of a fiddler to play on the kit, so that if you will not yield the sooner, I will ravish thee ere long with my music. Tis true I never gave thee a token but I have here sent you one I bought in the Exchange where all the folks hooted at me, but thought I, hoot and be hanged an you will so I buy a Top Knot for Joan; it will make a better show in church than a green bay leaf by thy side.

But what wilt thou give me for that, Joan? Alas, I ask nothing but thyself; come, Joan, give me thyself. Law ye what a happy day that would be, to see thee with thy best clothes on, at Church, and the Parson saying, I, Hodge, take thee Joan, and by the Mass I would take thee and hug thee and hug thee and buss thee, and then away to the Alehouse and hey for the Musicianers and the Canaries and the Sillybubs, and the Shoulder of Mutton and Gravy; and so having no more to say, I rest assured of your own good will

     Thy own dear sweetheart truly
          ROGER

Letter from Roger Prichard to the Birmingham Monthly Meeting of the Society of Friends.

     Almeley, 4th of ye 2nd. Mo. 1745
"To Friends of Ye Monthly Meeting in Birmingham or elsewhere:
I doe Permitt the bearer here of Jonathan Freeth too propose his intention of marriage with my Daughter Elizabeth Prichard according to the good order of Friends. In that behalfe as Witness my hand.
     ROGER PRICHARD."

"Respected Friend Unknown:

I understand by my son that he hath made proposition of marriage to thy Daughter. Being Recommended to ye family by my Cozon Swan of London Whose Carector of you is such that we are very well satisfied in and Desire only to be Conferred with, And very well approved of What my sone has done and if it be the will of ye Lord to bring it to pass that they may be a Comfort and a blessing to each other. I have herewith sent the particulars of my Estate What I am willing to grant into my sons hands at present and also after my days which I question not but will answer ye particularly to satisfaction Upon survay which I had Rather should be yr not. I understand my son hath given an Account of his brothers and sisters and what I expect for them on his settlement. My son is desirous to come over as soon as it may be thought convenient by you for if ye matter be put forward and agreed to he may come upon the Estate at Candlemas next I must Confess I Run to fast in this proposition not knowing whether my son may gain upon the Daughter's Affection. So leave it to they serious Consideration. My son desires to be kindly Remembered to you all especially to they Daughter Elizabeth and sends you hearty thanks for his kind entertainment with you. Will you be pleased to Eccept ye same to thyself from they

    Lo ffriend EDW. PRICHARD."

James Boswell is better known by his "Life of Johnson." than by his own life. The following letter is addressed to the daughter of a prominent Dutch family whom he met while studying in Utrecht. The girl turned him down. Who can blame her?

James Boswell to Isabella de Zuylen

Berlin, 9 July, 1764

My dear Zelide,

Be not angry with me for not writing to my fair friend before now. You know I am a man of form, a man who says to himself, Thus will I act, and acts accordingly. In short, a man subjected to discipline, who has his *orders* for his conduct during the day with as much exactness as any soldier in any service. And who gives these orders? I give them. Boswell when cool and sedate fixes rules for Boswell to live by in the common course of life, when perhaps Boswell might be dissipated and forget the distinctions between right and wrong, between propriety and impropriety. I own to you that this method of living according to a plan may sometimes be inconvenient and may even cause me to err. When such a man as I am, employs his great judgment to regulate small matters, methinks he resembles a giant washing teacups or threading a needle, both of which operations would be much better performed by a pretty little miss. There now is a pompous affectation of dignity; you must expect a good deal of this from me; but you have indeed seen me often enough not to be suprised at it . . . It was part of my system not to write to Zelide till my journey should be over. By my following that system, you must be almost four weeks without hearing a word from me. I will not pretend to doubt of your being sorry at this. I have even vanity enough to make me view you in tender attitudes of anxiety, such, however, as becomes a friend. Love is a passion which you and I have no thought of, at least for each other. . . . I am just a gentleman upon his travels, who has taken an attachment to you and who has your happiness at heart. I may add, a gentleman whom you honour with your esteem. My dear Zelide: You are very good, you are very candid. Pray, forgive me for begging you to be less vain. You have fine talents of one kind; but are you deficient in others? Do you think your *reason* is as distinguished as your imagination? Believe me, Zelide, it is not. Believe me and endeavour to improve . . .

You tell me, "Je ne vaudrois rien pour votre femme, je n'ai pas les talents subalternes." If by these talents you mean the domestic virtues you will find them necessary for the wife of every sensible man. But there are many stronger reasons against your being my wife; so strong that, as I said to you formerly, I would not be married to you to be a king. I know myself and I know you. And from all probability of reasoning, I am very certain that if we were married together, it would not be long before we should both be very miserable. My wife must have a character directly opposite to my dear Zelide, except in affection, in honesty, and in good humour . . .

Defend yourself. Tell me that I am the severe Cato. Tell me that you will make a very good wife. Let me ask you then, Zelide, could you submit your inclinations to the opinion, perhaps the *caprice* of a husband? Could you do this with cheerfulness, without losing any of your sweet good humour, without boasting of it? Could you live quietly in the country six months of the year? Could you make yourself agreeable to plain honest neighbours? . . . Could you live thus and be content, could you have a great deal of amusement in your own family? Could you give spirits to your husband when he is melancholy? I have known such wives, Zelide. What think you? Could you be such a one? If you can, you may be happy with the sort of man I once described to you. Adieu.

Laurence Sterne introduced into the language and into literature a new word—"sentimental"—which he used to describe a state of tender emotion with which he was especially familiar. He first used it in a letter to his future wife, Elizabeth Lumley, who eventually went insane because Sterne was "always miserably in love with someone outside of the domestic circle." While she was living in France, an invalid, he wrote to Eliza Draper, wife of an elderly government official in India; home on a visit. She fell for the charm of the famous author.

Laurence Sterne to Eliza Draper   *1767*

I wish to God, Eliza, it was possible to postpone the voyage to India for another year— You owe much, I allow, to your husband; you owe something to your appearance and the opinion of the world; but trust me, my dear, you owe much likewise to yourself. . . . I will send for my wife and daughter and they shall carry you in pursuit of health to Montpellier, the wells of Bancois, the Spa or whither thou wilt. Thou shalt direct them and make parties of pleasure in what corner of the world fancy points out to thee. We shall fish upon the banks of Arno, and lose ourselves in the sweet labyrinths of its valleys. . . . Indeed I begin to think you have as many virtues as my uncle Toby's widow. Talking of widows—pray, Eliza, if ever you are such, do not think of giving yourself to some wealthy Nabob

—because I design to marry you myself. My wife cannot live long—she has sold all the provinces in France already—I know not the woman I should like so well for her substitute as yourself. 'Tis true I am ninety-five in constitution, and you but twenty-five —rather too great a disparity this!—but what I want in youth I will make up in wit and good humor. Not Swift so loved his Stella, Scarron his Maintenon or Waller his Saccharissa, as I will love and sing thee, my wife elect! And those names, eminent as they were, shall give place to thine, Eliza. Tell me in answer to this that you approve and honor the proposal; and that you would (like the Spectator's mistress) have more joy in putting on an old man's slippers than associating with the gay, the voluptuous and the young.
    Adieu! by Simplicia!
     Yours
      TRISTRAM

Friedrich Schiller, German poet, was for some time equally devoted to both the sisters Lengefeld, Karoline and Charlotte. He could not make up his mind, till Karoline, the elder sister, made up his mind for him and decided that he should marry Lotte, the younger one. Three years after he had been introduced to them he married Lotte and they lived happily ever after.

Friedrich Schiller to Charlotte von Lengefeld

Leipzig, August 3, 1789

Is it true, dearest Lotte? May I hope Caroline has read in your soul and answered me from your heart the question I did not dare to put myself? Oh, how heavy this secret has become—I have kept it as long as we know each other. Often, while we were living in the same house I came to you, resolved to reveal it to you—but my courage left me. I thought I was selfish in my desires . . . considering only my own happiness . . . If I could not mean to you what you meant to me I might have destroyed the harmony of our friendship through my confession. And yet there were moments when my hopes rose again . . . when I even thought it noble to bring you all the rest as a sacrifice. You might be happy without me—you could never be unhappy through me. You might give yourself to another, but none could love you more purely or tenderly than I. To no one could your happiness be more sacred than it was and always will be to me. I dedicate my very existence and everything in me, everything, my dearest, to you, and if I strive to make myself more noble, it is only to make myself more worthy of you, to make you happier. Our friendship and love will be indestructible and eternal, like the feelings on which they are based.

. . . Tell me that everything that Caroline let me hope is true. Tell me that you will be mine, and that my happiness will cost you no sacrifice. Oh! Assure me of this, and with but a single word. Our hearts have been neighbors for long. Let us break down that single partition that stands between us and let nothing stand between the free communication of our souls.

Farewell, my dearest Lotte. I long for a calm moment to describe to you all the feelings of my heart which have made me so happy and again so unhappy, during the long time that this *one* longing has been in my soul. How much I still have to say!

Do not delay in banishing forever my unrest. I consign all the joys of my life to you. I can think of my joys under no other form than your image. Farewell, my dearest.

              SCHILLER

Sir Walter Scott had been very much in love with a young girl who married some one else. His proposal to Charlotte Carpenter (Charpentier), the daughter of a French refugee, was accepted. She made him a good wife, but his affection for her was more of the rational than of the passionate sort. He took it out in his novels where he put all the romance that life had denied him.

Sir Walter Scott to Charlotte Carpenter   1797

Since Miss Carpenter has forbid my seeing her for the present, I am willing to incur even the hazard of her displeasure by intruding upon her in this manner. My anxiety, which is greater than I can find words to express, leads me to risque what I am sure if you could but know my present (condition) would not make you very, very angry.

Gladly would I have come to Carlisle to-morrow, and returned here to dinner; but dearly as I love my friend, I would ever sacrifice my own personal gratification to follow the line of conduct which is most agreeable to her. I likewise wish to enter more particularly into the circumstances of my situation, which I should most heartily despise myself were I capable of concealing or misrepresenting to you. Being only the second brother of a large family, you will easily conceive that tho' my father is a man in easy circumstances, my success in life must depend upon my own exertions. This I have been always taught to expect, and far from considering it as a hardship, my feelings on that subject have ever been those of confidence in myself.

Hitherto, from reasons which have long thrown a lassitude over my mind, to which it is not naturally liable, my professional exertions have been culpably neglected; and as I reside with my father, I gave myself little trouble, provided my private income did but answer my personal expense and the maintenance of a horse or two. At the some time, none of those who were called to the Bar with myself can boast of having very far outstripped me in the career of life or of business.

I have every reason to expect that the Sheriffdom of a particular County, presently occupied by a gentleman in a very precarious state of health, may soon fall to my lot. The salary is 250 pounds per annum, and the duty does not interfere with the exercise of my profession, but greatly advances it . . . Many other little resources, which I cannot easily explain so as to make you comprehend me, induce me to express myself with confidence upon the probability of my success; and oh, how dear these prospects will become to me would my beloved friend but permit me to think that she would share them!

If you could form any idea of the society in Edinburgh, I am sure the prospect of living there would not terrify you. Your situation would entitle you to take as great a share in the amusements of the place as you were disposed to; and when you were tired of these, it should be the study of my life to prevent your feeling one moment's *Ennui*. When care comes, we will laugh it away; or if the load is too heavy, we will sit down and share it between us, till it becomes almost as light as pleasure itself. You are apprehensive of losing your liberty; but could you but think with how many domestic pleasures the sacrifice will be repaid, you would no longer think it very frightful. Indisposition may deprive you of that liberty which you prize so highly, and age certainly will. Oh, think how much happier you will find yourself, surrounded by friends who will love you, than with those who will only regard even my beloved Charlotte while she possesses the power of interesting or entertaining them.

You seem, too, to doubt the strength, or at least the stability, of my affection; I can only protest to you most solemnly that a truer never warmed a mortal's breast, and that though it may appear sudden it is not rashly adopted. You yourself must allow that from the nature of our acquaintance, we are entitled to judge more absolutely of each other, than from a much longer one trammelled with the usual forms of life; and tho' I have been repeatedly in similar situations with amiable and accomplished women, the feelings I entertain for you have ever been strangers to my bosom, except during a period I have often alluded to.

I have settled in my mind to see you on Monday

next. I stay thus long to give you time to make what inquiries you may think proper, and also because you seemed to wish it. All Westmoreland and Cumberland shall not detain me a minute longer. In the meanwhile I do not expect you to write. You shall do nothing to commit yourself. How this week will pass away I know not; but a more restless, anxious being never numbered the hours than I have been this whole day. Do not think of bidding me *forget you,* when we again meet — Oh, do not; the thing is really impossible, as impossible as it is to express how much I love you, and how truly I believe our hearts were formed for each other. Mr. and Mrs. B. are Hospitality itself, but all will not do. I would fain make you laugh before concluding, but my heart is rather too full for trifling. Adieu, adieu, souvenez-vous de moi.

W. Scott

Gerhard Leberecht von Blücher, German Field Marshal who, with Wellington, conquered Napoleon, had lost his wife in 1791 and proposed to the very wealthy Frau von S., as follows, in March, 1795. But on April 1 he withdrew his proposal "because of too unequal fortunes." He later married a girl thirty years younger than he, Amalie von Colomb, and was very happy with her.

Field Marshal Blücher to Frau von S.   *1795*

Most gracious lady!

I acknowledge the sentiments which you have expressed for me, gratefully and respectfully. My silence is unpardonable; but I am too honorable and it is just this which justifies my conduct. I have never yet deceived anyone; I should like least of all to deceive you. Well, to business!

1. How can I ask you to marry me, when all my affairs are topsy-turvy, and I am in debt to the extent of 5000 dollars? To be sure, my prospects are good; I have a good job which can support me fairly well. But we cannot count on its permanence.

2. I have three children whom I love. Their mother made me her heir but I gave up the inheritance in favor of my beloved children. My children are well taken care of; but I have nothing.

3. I am not much of a hand at saving money. Liv-

ing with my officers, helping my subalterns when they need money—this makes me happy. But I cannot get rich at it.

4. I can't enter upon any marriage which does not make provision for my old age and for the welfare of my children. Please understand me correctly; I am a long way from asking that the lady who grants me her hand in marriage should also turn over to me her income for the rest of her life; far from it! But your income will have to be added to mine, so that I may be in a position to maintain my social standing, character, and wife properly. I am aware, dear lady, that you are the possessor of a considerable income; your feelings for me are tender; your magnanimity cannot exceed my gratitude. Well then! If you are resolved to make me happy—my hand and heart are at your feet. If, as I sincerely hope, you outlive me, do not count on my leaving any wealth behind because I possess none.

Dear Lady; you have here my frank and honest confession of faith; treat me in a similar manner! Tell me what you intend to do for me. I will take infinite pains to deserve your love and friendship, and will always strive to keep you from regretting your decision to marry me. There is just one more thing I must mention: I have a daughter ten years of age, whom I idolize. I shall give this child into your arms and humbly beseech you to watch over her rearing, since you yourself already have the perfection that I should like to see her attain . . .

Honor me with a speedy answer! Let me know where I stand! And count on the unbounded respect of him who loves and honors you

BLUECHER

Napoleon's proposal to the Archduchess of Austria is very Empire. Ten years earlier he had written baroque letters of passion to Josephine; but he needed a son for succession, and so, at the peak of his power he divorced her and was accepted by the Hapsburg princess. She did not love him, but she gave him the heir to the crown, who bore the title of a "King of Rome". When Napoleon was exiled she attached herself to the Count Neipperg whom she married after Napoleon's death in 1821. The son died as a young boy.

Emperor Napoleon I to the Archduchess Maria Louise of Austria   Rambouillet, February 23, 1810

Dear Cousin,

The striking qualities which enhance your person have inspired in us the desire to serve and honor you.

We are requesting the Emperor, your respected father, to entrust to us the happiness of Your Imperial Highness.

May we be permitted to hope that you will receive graciously the feelings which impel us to take this step? May we harbor the flattering hope that you will agree to this marriage not only because of filial obedience and duty?

If Your Imperial Highness has but the slightest affection for us we will cultivate this feeling with the greatest pains, and make it our supreme task ever to seek your happiness in every respect. In this way we fondly hope to win your complete affection some day. That is our most fervent wish, and we beg your Imperial Highness to be favorably inclined to us.

NAPOLEON

Augustus Frederick, Duke of Sussex, sixth son of George III, far enough from succession to the throne, was happier than other princes in that he could marry a commoner without upsetting world affairs. He had met Lady Augusta Murray in Rome. She was six years older that he and refused his first proposals in his own interest; but he persisted, got hold of Mr. Gunn, a minister of the Church of England resident in Rome, made him promise to perform the marriage ceremony and went on a hunger-strike as shown by his letter. It proved successful.

Augustus Frederick, Duke of Sussex, to Lady Augusta Murray   Rome, 1820

Will you allow me to come this evening? It is my only hope. Oh let me come and we will send for Mr. Gunn. Everything but this is hateful to me. More than forty-eight hours have passed without my taking the smallest nourishment. Oh let me not live so. Death is certainly better than this—which if in forty-eight hours it has not occurred must follow; for by all that is holy, till I am married I will eat nothing, and if I am not married the promise will die with me. I am resolute. Nothing shall alter my resolution. If Gunn will not marry me I shall die . . .

Prince William of Prussia, who, with Bismarck as his chancellor, united, as William I. the quibbling tribes of Northern Europe into the German Reich, had been passionately in love with Princess Elizabeth Radziwill, but he had to give her up because the King, his father, put his foot down and said No. His letter to the Weimarian Princess is Empire style, and the relations, when they married, were of the same cool and formal kind. But she was a good Empress and played her part as best she could.

Prince William of Prussia (later William I) of Hohenzollern to Princess Augusta of Saxe-Weimar

Berlin, August, 1828

I can scarcely describe to your Highness the excitement which fills my heart at this moment when I take my pen in hand to make the most important move of my life.

With trepidation, but also with the assurance that God will be near me in this decisive moment, I approach you with confidence.

Your Highness herself has inspired this feeling of confidence in me; but many other feelings are closely connected with this one to make you inexpressibly dear to me and to bind me to you forever—if your Highness will grant me your gracious consent. To learn whether I may expect this consent, whether I may see my fondest wishes fulfilled and count on a response to those feelings—to settle the uncertainty in my heart, may I expect your Highness' decision and answer?

If my heart has not deceived me, I may receive from you a confirmation of my hopes. If God grants me his favor, I shall hasten, grateful to him and to you, to lay my gratitude at your feet in person.

I sign myself as
>> Your Highness' most devoted servant
>> WILHELM, *Prince of Prussia*

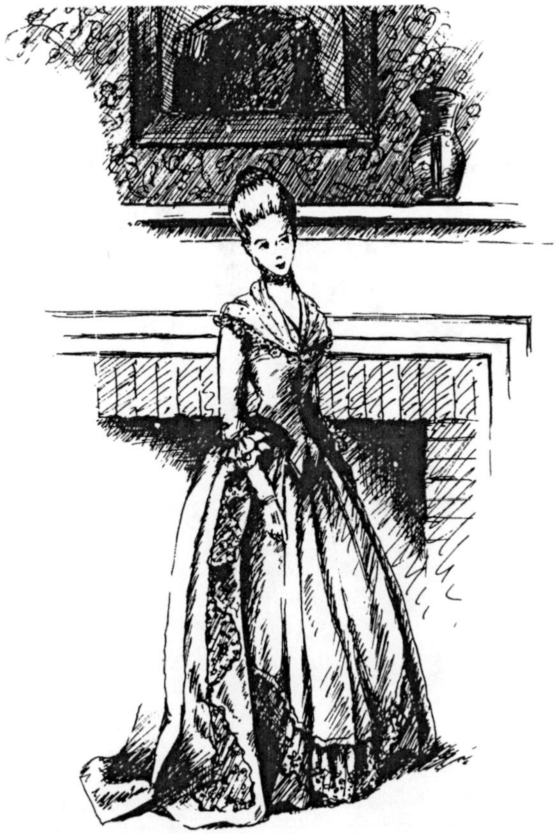

The Victorians

(ECLECTIC)

THE VICTORIAN AGE was eclectic in its mixture of styles and in its constant swing of the pendulum between understatement and overstatement. It yields more proposal letters than any other age. Most of them are long and wordy. A small choice of them will show the trend, in strong contrast to what follows in the Twentieth Century, the Modern Age, the Functional Age.

William Hazlitt, famous essayist, started his career as a painter, became a friend of the lake poets, Coleridge and Wordsworth. He wooed Sarah Stoddard, Mary Lamb's friend, in very simple language.

They married, but Hazlitt seems to have been a better essayist than husband. They were divorced in 1822. Two years later he married Mrs. Bridgewater. This unison did not last beyond a year's travel on the continent.

William Hazlitt to Sarah Stoddard.
... I would not give a pin for a girl whose cheeks never tingle—nor for myself if I could not make them tingle, sometimes. Now, though I always am writing to you about "lips and noses" and such sort of stuff, yet as I sit by my fireside (which I generally do eight or ten hours a day) I often think of you in a more serious and sober light. For indeed I never love you so well as when I think of sitting with you to dinner on a broiled scragg-end of mutton and hot potatoes. You then please my fancy more than when I think of you in . . . no, you would never forgive me if I were to finish the sentence. Now I think of it, what do you mean to be dressed in when we are married? But it does not much matter. I wish you would let your hair grow; though perhaps nothing will be better than "the same air and look with which at first my heart was took."

Charles Lamb, essayist, famous through the "Tales from Shakespeare" which he wrote with his sister Mary, proposed, late in life, to the actress, Miss Kelly.

She said no—she was in love with some one else. But they remained friends.

1819

Dear Miss Kelly,

We had the pleasure, pain I might better call it, of seeing you last night in the new play. It was a most consummate piece of acting, but what a task for you to undergo, at a time when your heart is sore with real sorrow. It has given rise to a train of thinking which I cannot suppress.

Would to God you were released from this way of life—that you could bring your mind to consent to take your lot with us, and throw off for ever the whole burden of your profession . . . I neither expect nor wish you to take notice of that which I am writing in your present over-occupied and hurried state, but to think of it at your leizure. I have quite income enough, if that were all, to justify my making a proposal, with what I may call even a handsome provision for my survivor. What you possess of your own would naturally be apportioned to those for whose sakes chiefly you have made so many hard sacrifices. I am not so foolish as not to know that I am a most unworthy match for such a one as you, but you have for years been a principal object of my mind. In many a sweet assumed character have I learned to love you, but simply as F. M. Kelly I love you better than them all. Can you quit these shadows of existence and come and be reality to us? Can you leave off harrassing yourself to please a thankless multitude who knows nothing of you, and begin at last to live for yourself and your friends?

In haste, but with entire respect and deepest affection

CHARLES LAMB

The great composer Robert Schumann, when studying music in Leipzig with Friedrich Wieck, the pianist, came to an affectionate understanding with his teacher's daughter Clara. His proposal was turned down because of his uncertain future. After taking his degree he married the girl against her father's will. Sixteen years later he died insane; Clara lived forty years longer and helped Johannes Brahms through years of a devoted friendship.

Robert Schumann to Friedrich Wieck (for his daughter, Clara Wieck)   *September 13, 1837*

What I have to say to you is so simple—and yet the right words won't come. A trembling hand cannot guide a pen calmly. If I make some mistakes in grammar or expression, I beg your indulgence.

Today is Clara's birthday—the day on which the dearest thing on earth to me and to you first saw the light of this world . . . If I say so myself, I have never viewed my future prospects so calmly as I do today. Securely fixed against need, so far as my human understanding can predict, ambitious ideas in my head, a heart moved to enthusiasm by everything noble, hands ready for work, conscious of the great effect I shall have, and still hopeful of doing everything that can be expected of my powers, honored and loved by many—I should think that would be enough! Oh! the painful answer I must give myself! What is all that, compared to the pain of being separated from the one being who makes all this striving worthwhile, and who returns my love truly and ardently. You know this being, you happy father, only too well. Ask her eyes if I have spoken the truth!

You tested me for eighteen months, as rigorously as Fate itself. I hurt you deeply, but you have let me atone for it. Now test me again as long. Perhaps, if you not demand the impossible, my powers will keep pace with your desires; perhaps I shall gain your confidence again. You know I am persistent in matters of importance. If you find me capable, then bless this union of two souls, for whose greatest happiness nothing is lacking but parental blessing. It is not the excitement of the moment, not passion, nothing superficial that binds me to Clara with all the fibers of my being. It is the deep conviction that no marriage has ever been prepared under such a favorable harmony of circumstances, it is this adorable girl herself who radiates happiness and who guarantees ours. If you are also convinced of this, then give me a definite promise that for the time being you will decide nothing about Clara's future, as I give you my word not to speak to Clara against your wishes. Grant us just one thing, that when you go on lengthy trips, we may keep each other informed. . . .

With the deepest emotion of which an oppressed,

loving heart is capable, I implore you: Give us your blessing, be once more a friend to one of your oldest friends, and to the best child in the world be the best father!

ROBERT SCHUMANN

Otto von Bismarck, the "wild Junker," wrote this amazing letter to the pietist Puttkamer. Johanna became, as his wife, the symbol of the German Hausfrau; she gave him a happy homelife and the calm relaxation that his demonic temperament needed. That the Iron Chancellor should have looked upon his early life in the way he makes out in his letter will be a revelation to those who idolize his memory as well as to those who hate what he stood for.

Prince Otto von Bismarck, later Chancellor of the German Reich, to the father of his future wife 1846

Most honored Herr von Puttkamer!

I begin this letter by indicating its contents; it is to ask you for the supreme thing that you can give away in this world: the hand of your daughter. I know I seem audacious if, known to you only recently and from sparse meetings, I ask you for the highest proof of trust that you can give to a man. I also know that, apart from all handicaps of space and time which might make it difficult for you to form an opinion of me, I shall by myself never be able to give you such security for the future as would warrant the handing over of such a precious pledge, unless you complete by faith in God what faith in man cannot do. What I can do is limited to my giving you information about myself with unreserved openness, so far as I have reached clarity about myself. You can easily get reports about my outward behavior from others; therefore I shall only give a description of my inner life, which is its base, and especially about my attitude towards Christianity.

I must go far back. I had early become a stranger to my parents' home and never felt completely at home there afterwards, and my education was carried out with a view to developing first and foremost practical reasoning and to submitting everything else to the acquisition of practical knowledge as early as possible. After irregularly attended and uncomprehended religious instruction I was confirmed by Schleirmacher on my sixteenth birthday; I had at that time no other religion except a naked deism which did not remain long without an admixture of pantheism. It was about this time that I stopped saying my evening prayer as I had been accustomed to do from childhood; for praying seemed to me to be in contradiction to my view of God, who either by Himself, according to His omnipresence, was producing all my thoughts and my will—and, therefore, was praying through me to Himself—or if my will was independent of God's will it would be presumptuous and indicate doubt in God's eternal constancy and the unchangeable completeness of His decisions if one tried to influence Him by prayer. Not quite seventeen, I went to the University of Gottingen. For eight years I rarely saw my parents' house. My father leniently left me alone; my mother, from a distance, rebuked me if I neglected my studies and professional work and obviously thought she could leave the rest to higher guidance. Apart from this the teaching and advice from others did not reach me. If in this period studies which ambition at times drove me to, or disgust with the emptiness of my life, brought me into contact with serious life and eternity, I looked into the philosophies of the ancients, or Hegel's half-understood writings, but first and foremost the mathematical clarity of Spinoza for reassurance about what human reason cannot grasp. To intensive thinking about this I only came through solitude when, after my mother's death six or seven years ago, I moved to Kniephof. Though my views did not change materially there in the beginning, an inner voice soon began to be audible in the solitude and to show me many things as wrong which I had thought permissible before. But always my endeavor towards understanding remained bound by the circle of reason, and led me through the reading of Strauss, Feuerbach, Bruno, Bauer, only deeper into the dead end path of doubt. I came to the conclusion that God has denied man the possibility of understanding and that it was arrogance to pretend to know the will and the way of the Lord; that man must await in devotion what his Creator would decide about him in death, and that His will cannot be known to us on earth except through the voice of our conscience which He has given us as a cornucopia through the darkness of the world. That I did not find peace in this faith I need not say; I passed many hours of disconsolate depression in the thought that my own and other people's existence was without aim and use, perhaps just a chance by-product of creation, coming and going, like dust rolling off the wheels.

Four years ago I met, for the first time since my school days, Moritz Blankenburg and found in him what I had never before had in my life: a friend; the warm zeal of his love tried in vain to give me, in discussions and talks, what I lacked: faith. But in his circle I found people who made me feel ashamed because I had tried with the poor light of my reason to probe into things which superior minds had accepted as true and sacred in childlike faith. I saw the members of this circle to be in their outward actions almost invariably examples of what I wished to be. I was not surprised to see that they had peace and trust because I had never doubted that peace and trust were companions of faith; but faith cannot be given or taken—I felt I should have to wait to see whether it would come to me. But I felt happy in this circle with a happiness never felt before; I had a family to which I belonged, almost a home. . . .

I came, through others and by my own urge, to read the Bible, and what stirred in me came to life when our dear late friend in Cardemin fell fatally ill. My first prayer since childhood days was for her and though God has not granted it, He has not turned it down for I have not lost again the capacity for asking Him and I feel, if not peace, faith and courage for life as I for long had not known it.

I do not know how you will value these feelings only two months old but I hope I shall not lose them whatever shall be decided about my proposal, a hope which I could not assure you of otherwise than by my complete frankness and loyalty in what I have told you and nobody else, in the faith that God gives success to the loyal.

I refrain from every expression of feeling and intention as regards your daughter for the step I am undertaking talks louder and more eloquently than words. Neither can promises for the future be of any use for you know better than I the unreliability of the human heart. The only security for your daughter's welfare lies in my prayer for the blessing of the Lord. Historically I want to state that after I had seen Miss Johanna repeatedly in Cardemin, after our trip together this summer I was only in doubt whether the fulfilment of my wishes would be in harmony with the happiness and peace of your daughter, and whether my self-confidence were not greater than my power if I thought I possessed the qualities she was entitled to find in a husband. Recently, with my trust in God's grace, the decision has matured in me which I now carry through; I have been silent in Zimmerhausen only because I had more to say than I could say by word of mouth. . . .

I am sure there is much which I have not said or not made clear enough in this letter; I am prepared, of course, to give precise and honest information about everything you would want to know. The most important things I believe I have said.

Please give your wife my devoted regards and accept the assurance of my love and respect with kindness.

Bismarck

Thomas Carlyle was no match for Jane Welsh; she was young, beautiful and rich; he was a poor, highly nervous and erratic genius and lacked all the essential qualities for a good husband. Her mother was opposed to the marriage. They corresponded for years. Jane herself was an excellent translator of folklore and a writer of distinction whose work Carlyle much admired, even at the peak of his own fame. In the end Jane decided to become a poor man's wife. She settled her fortune on her mother and married him. Their life together was one hurricane of happiness and misery, their home in Chelsea, with all its material discomforts and spiritual luxuries, was a center for the intellectual life of London at the time.

Thomas Carlyle to Jane Welsh   *1823*

My dear Jane,

I have longed for the arrival of this day . . . your letter was waiting for me, to welcome me. And such a welcome! I felt in reading it and reading it again as if it were more to me than the charter to all the metal of Potosi. What a frank and true and noble spirit is my Jane's! No artifice, no vulgar management; her sentiments come warm and fearless from her heart because they are pure and honest as herself, and the friend whom she trusts she trusts without reserve. I often ask myself: Is not all this a dream? Is it true that the most enchanting creature I have ever seen does actually love me? No! Thank God it is not a dream; Jane loves me! She loves me! and I swear by the Immortal Powers that she shall yet be mine, as I am hers, through life and death and all the dark vicissitudes that wait us here and hereafter. In more reasonable moments I perceive that I am very selfish and almost mad. Alas! My fate is dreary and perilous and obscure; is it fit that you whom I honour among the fairest of God's words, whom I love more dearly than my own soul, should partake of it? . . . If I were intellectual sovereign of all the world, if I were—but it is vain to speculate. I know that I am nothing. I know not that I shall not always be so. The only thing I know is that you are the most delightful, enthusiastic, contemptuous, capricious, affectionate, sarcastic, warmhearted, lofty-minded half-devil, half-angel of a woman that ever ruled over the heart of a man; that I will love you, must love you, whatever betide, till the last moment of my existence, and that if we both act rightly our lot *may* be the happiest of a thousand mortal lots. So let us cling to one another (if you dare, if thus forewarned)—forever and ever! . . . You will yet be blessed yourself in making me more blessed than man has right to look for being upon earth. God bless you, my heart's darling!

Victor Hugo, who in his later life scarcely could have been called Victorian, exhibited some of the style of his namesake on the British throne in his early love-making. His young fiancée, Adele Faucher, had offered to live with him, should his father refuse to permit their marriage. She preferred living in sin to having her boy-friend go crazy as his brother Eugene did. His letter is written while he was waiting for his father's permission. They were married, and Eugene, also in love with Adele, went to the madhouse and died there. Victor became rich, famous and highly influential in the political life of France, but the harmony of his married life was disturbed by his amorous escapades which often proved more sensational, dramatic and fantastic than even his plays and novels.

Victor Hugo to Adele Faucher   1822

Adele, to what follies, to what delirium did not your Victor give way . . . sometimes I was ready to accept your offer; . . . I thought we would go across France . . . by day we would travel in the same carriage, by night sleep under the same roof. But do not think, my noble Adele, that I would have taken advantage of so much happiness . . . you would have been the object of the most worthy respect . . . you might on the journey even have slept in the same chamber without fearing that I would have alarmed you by a touch or have even looked at you. I would have slept, or watched wakefully, on a chair or lying on the floor beside your bed, the guardian of your repose, the protector of your slumbers.

The letter of proposal not for marriage that the Austrian playwright Johann Nestroy wrote to a lady of light reputation has found place here because it is unique. The writer did not sign his name; he added 'von' to his pseudonym, to appear to be of the nobility, because he probably presumed that might impress the lady more than his other "attractions."

Johann Nestroy to Fräulein Koefer (but not for marriage)   *March 12, 1855*

To Fräulein von Koefer,
    Stadt, Schultergasse 402
        on the third floor.
Mine Fräulein!

Not only this letter in itself, but also its length will amaze you (I risk it, as I risk its complete lack of success). I will not tire your patience by the usual lengthy excuses but come straight to the point.

I never spend an evening without going to the theater. Therefore I have seen you repeatedly. I do not think I was happy enough to be noticed by you—one is generally unnoticed if one presents oneself with one's missus, chained in marriage (though perhaps otherwise not without attractions). One time a couple of dandies in the second box from mine, were the aim of your opera glasses and the subject of my secret envy.

I dare express in these lines what you must have heard from others, and often: that you are in the highest degree attractive, interesting and the object of my most passionate desires.

How are you going to take these words? Maybe you will laugh at me as an impudent, unknown 'man. Maybe if you have a lover—and it is almost unthinkable that you should not have one—you will laugh at me with him. Then I can console myself with the thought that you might not have laughed had you known me.

I do not know your conditions of life. I have most strictly forbidden my man-servant who followed you going home and found out your name from a fellow standing on the stairs (he was very unfriendly) every further curiosity which might have hurt your feelings if you had heard about it. My opinion is: beautiful young ladies in whatever circumstances of life ought not to turn down a discreet friend male secretly happy and immensely grateful. Even if you should be engaged to be married, such a secret friend might not be without use to you after the honeymoon. If you agree I hope you will not refuse my proposal. . . .

I shall choose a harmless hour—two o'clock in the afternoon—and a harmless location—the main Avenue in the Prater. Tomorrow at half past one I shall be riding from the lower end of the Avenue to its upper end, the Praterstern. If you, at the same time, will ride from the Praterstern to the Rondeau, our carriages will pass each other. Please hold your handkerchief out of the right window of your carriage (seeing we drive on the left in Vienna) so that I can recognize your carriage from a distance. This handkerchief will be the thrilling sign for me that, in case you find me worthy of your affection, you will agree to my views as expressed above about a secret liaison.

As many carriages pass the Corso at this time I shall make myself known to you by a light grey traveling-coat piped with red. I shall not attempt to follow you, but I will take your appearance as permission for the next step which I am going to take. That will be another letter which you will receive on the following day (Friday). In that I shall propose the place and time where we shall meet and talk with each other . . . I should suggest next Sunday as the day.

Your devoted admirer
L. B. von R.

Leo Nikolajewitsch Tolstoi, great Russian poet and life reformer, as a mature man, lost his heart to Sophie Behr, daughter of a physician. The family thought he was in love with her elder sister, till he, in this intense, shy and almost hysterical way, proposed—he was visiting with them and he could never muster courage to talk to her. She accepted him. Their married life was an adventure of storms and revolutions up to the moment when he, an old man, left his home to go and die in complete solitude.

Count Leo Tolstoi to Sonya Behr   1862

Sophie Andreyevna, it is becoming unbearable. For three weeks I've been saying to myself: "I shall tell her now," and yet I continue to go away with the same feeling of sadness, regret, terror, and happiness in my heart. Every night I go over the past and curse myself for not having spoken to you, and wonder what I would have said if I *had* spoken. I am taking this letter with me, in order to hand it to you should my courage fail me again. Your family have the false notion, I believe, that I am in love with Lisa. This is quite wrong. Your story has clung to my mind because, after reading it, I have come to the conclusion that "Prince Dublitzky" has no right to think of happiness, and that your poetic view of love is different . . . that I am not jealous, and must not be jealous, of the man you will love. I thought I could love you all like children. I wrote at Ivitsy,

"Your presence reminds me too vividly of my old age" —*you r* presence in particular. But then, as now, I was lying to myself. At Ivitsy I might still have been able to break away and to return to my hermitage, back to my solitary work and my absorbing labors. Now I can't do anything; I feel I have created a disturbance in your home, and that your friendship for me, as a good, honorable man, has also been spoiled. I dare not leave and I dare not stay. You are a candid, honest girl; with your hand on your heart, and without hurrying (for God's sake, don't hurry!), tell me what to do. I would have laughed myself sick a month ago if I had been told that I would suffer, suffer joyfully, as I have been doing for this past month. Tell me, with all the candor that is yours: Will you be my wife? If you can say *yes, boldly,* with all your heart, then *say it;* but if you have the faintest shadow of doubt, say *no.* For heaven's sake, think it over carefully. I am terrified to think of a *no,* but I am prepared for it and will be strong enough to bear it. But it will be terrible if I am not loved by my wife as much as I love you!

Anton Bruckner, Austrian composer of beautiful symphonies, was shy and clumsy in everything but music. Women turned him down, politely and rudely. He used to say, plaintively: "No girl will have me." He never married.

Anton Bruckner to Josefine Lang
Most honored and amiable Fräulein,

The matter with which I turn to you should not surprise you; no, I am sure that you have long been aware of my constant waiting for you, and so I take up my pen to trouble you. The great and profound request which I take the liberty to address to you herewith, Fräulein Josefine, is this: would Fräulein Josefine kindly give her frank final and decisive answer, in writing, for my future calm, to the question: May I hope and ask your dear parents for your hand? or is it impossible for you to marry me, for lack of affection? Fräulein must see that the question is of utmost importance to me, so I beg you to write as soon as possible the one way or the other, resolutely and decisively. Please may Fräulein Josefine tell this to no one but her parents (please to preserve the strictest secrecy) and take your choice between the two points of the question in agreement with your dear parents. My loyal friend, your honored brother, has already prepared me for everything and has, according to his promise, informed you. Once more I beg you: write frankly and sincerely:

either that I may propose, or a complete and permanent refusal, (please no compromise to console or evade the point, for it is high time for me) and your feelings will probably not change because Fräulein is reasonable. Fräulein Josefine may say the whole truth without fear because in any case it will give me peace of mind.

Expecting a decisive answer as soon as possible, I kiss your hand.

ANTON BRUCKNER

Friedrich Nietzsche, philosopher of the superman theory, which has been made partly responsible for recent developments in Germany, must have been rather meek in his marriage ambitions. His letter to Miss Trampedach who had planned to copy Longfellow's poem "Excelsior" for him, lacks the dynamic qualities he described in his ideal "Herrenmensch." Mathilde refused to become his superwife. She turned him down politely and married one of his friends, a musical conductor.

Friedrich Nietzsche to Mathilde Trampedach
Geneva, April 11, 1876

Mein Fräulein,

Tonight you are writing something for me—I should write something for you, too.

Summon all the courage of your heart in order not to be shocked by the question I shall put to you: Will you marry me?

I love you and I feel as if you belong to me already. Not a word about the suddenness of my affection. At least there is no guilt in it, and therefore nothing need be excused. But what I should like to know is whether you feel the same: that we have never been strangers to each other, not for a moment! Do you not also believe that, united, we could become freer and better than separate—excelsior? Will you risk going with me—

as with one who struggles valiantly for liberation and progress on all the paths of life and thought? Now be frank with me and keep nothing back; no one knows anything about this letter and my question except our mutual friend Herr von S.

I am leaving tomorrow for Basel. I have to go back. I enclose my Basel address. If you say yes to my question, I shall write to your mother at once. If you can decide quickly either way, a letter can reach me tomorrow until ten at the Hotel Garni de la Poste.

Wishing you every happiness and bliss forever,
FRIEDRICH NIETZSCHE

Adolf Stoecker, Court-Preacher to Wilhelm I. of Germany, was one of the early pacemakers for Hitler—the first propagator of Pan-germanism and its race theories. For preaching anti-semitism from the pulpit he was fired by the Emperor, but he went into politics and preached it from platform and soap box. When he asks his lady "in trembling and fear" and, like the early colonists, puts the whole responsibility for his sexual emotions on the Lord, one might well ask, whether his political shouting was overcompensated weakness, or whether he was just a hypocrite.

Adolf Stoecker, Court-Preacher and Propagator of Pan-germanism, to Anna Krueger
                              Seggerde, March 8, 1864

Highly Honoured Fräulein,

   I begin this letter with trembling and fear, because your answer to it will bring me the greatest happiness or the most abysmal grief. I fought and wrestled with myself for so long a time, at last after much praying and searching before God, I have found the courage to tell you that I love you with all my heart. I know full well that I ask something great and precious in asking you to love me in return. I also know that I do not deserve to call all this goodness and charm which my soul has discerned in you, my own. And yet I am compelled by an irresistible force to ask you in the name of the Lord, who has put this great and ardent love into my heart, whether you could reciprocate my affection.

From the first hour that I spent happily in your company, the thought has never left me that your love could make me completely happy—could lift me to Heaven on the wings of an angel and fulfill all my hopes and dreams—that, with you, I could build my house on the foundation of our living Saviour, trusting in our unity of faith, love and prayer.

Accept, then, hochverehrtes Fräulein, the secret of my life; may the Almighty accept it and weigh it in the hands of his Grace. My soul would exult if he would hear my prayer and incline your heart toward mine; His will be done.

In sincere love and affection

your
ADOLF

August Strindberg, Swedish dramatist, was born in Stockholm in 1849; his father was a small tradesman, his mother a barmaid. On the stage, as in real life, he rebelled against conventions. Marriage was one of them. He tried it three times, always without success. His first entanglement was Sigrid Wrangel, the wife of an army officer who divorced her husband to marry him in 1877. He separated from her and married Frieda (Pussy) Uhl, who now takes boarders in her little castle on an Austrian lake, while their son works as a newspaper man. His third failure was a Swedish actress, Harriet Bosse. He grew more and more bitter with every venture in the matrimonial field and took it out in vicious attacks between book covers and in plays.

August Strindberg to Frieda Uhl

Berlin, March 11, 1893

Dear, good, beautiful, nasty little thing—what are you doing in Munich? Come here to me, we'll put an end to all the gossip, exchange rings, pay our visits, and then we'll be betrothed. If you're afraid of getting married, we can wait a while and test ourselves. After all, a betrothal isn't a rigid bond. You long for me, don't you, and you are afraid it is all only a dream! It is not a dream, only the simple truth, that I love you—I love you, I love you.

It is not "purposeless" to come back to Berlin! You

will get a man who loves you and whom you need not despise. A man who will be loyal to you, whether he wants to or not, because you're so young and beautiful and clever and crazy. I even love all the perfectly mad things that you do: when you lie, you lie as only a poet, as only I can lie; I love you because your mouth is so beautiful and your little teeth are so pearly white; when you're angry I love you because your deep eyes spit fire; I love you because you're so horribly clever and greedy, because you write your disagreeable business letters for my sake.

And so: come here and live in the west, so I can live here, too, and I'll work, and love you until you are completely crazy.

Now you know everything! Good night, my darling,
Your
AUGUST STRINDBERG

August Strindberg to Regierungsrat Friedrich Uhl
Dear Sir,

Deeply regretting the indiscretion of the newspapers which published the engagement of Fräulein Frieda Uhl before I had had an opportunity of writing to you, I beg to ask your approval of this marriage.

An indisposition frustrated my hopes of calling on you in Vienna; it chained me to my bed during these last days.

As my affairs tie me to Berlin, I would like to ask you to permit your daughter to take up her residence here, as soon as possible, again, so that we can together prepare everything for the wedding which we wish to celebrate in May.

Looking forward to your kind answer, I beg you to believe in my gratitude and affection.

AUGUST STRINDBERG

The Moderns

THE MODERNS ARE FUNCTIONAL in their proposals. They show understatement driven to its extreme. Whatever young people of today feel, they do not show it. Control of emotions is the last word in style.

The letters in this section have, for obvious reasons, to be presented under fictitious names. Those who contributed them expected their privacy to be protected. Three of them were written by girls.

Letter writing is going out of practise—specially the writing of proposal letters. People wire or cable; they ring up long distance. Even the few who do write sound cryptic. Sam, the author of the first letter, insists that he did not write his proposal intentionally so that it could not be used as evidence in a breach of promise court; he only wanted to persuade his girl of the fact that he was a "long rope" and that being tied to him would be less uncomfortable than being tied to some one who has substituted his flower-pot soil for

24th of January, 1927

Dearest Ruth,

    ... people tied with a short rope have such a radius —and people with no attachment are disposed with infinity. But the human being demands some element of rope to keep from getting out of sight. If an individual has both a short rope and a long rope tied around his body, then the short rope is responsible for a lot of slack.

What kind of people are short ropes? Human flowers who can exist in only one flower pot—people who cannot stand to be disturbed and therefore have to be handled with gloves—people who have substituted their flower-pot soil for cement.

To cater to such people means a recoil. An elastic band stings the hand of the puller when the gripper lets go. The latter does not release intentionally. He lets go because of an innate vanity since his solidifying habits cannot stand the effect of the uncongealor. What kind of people are long ropes? I will sign one's name now.

SAM

Dear Carolus,

As I am going to say in my next letter. it certainly was sweet of you to fix the victrola when you left your room for me to use while you were away for Christmas —and then take away all the records! You were too much in a Christmas mood, I guess. My high spirits went back almost to the depths. Sorry about your gloves. I'd hid them away under the radio so that you would have to find me to get them.

Did I tell you I wanted to stay on here after Noël for a few days? Your landlady says you had not mentioned it. Is that OK? Or are you coming back early?

And you *would* write so that it'll get here tomorrow! And I'll be gone for a day and won't get it till after Christmas. Yeah, I know it's my fault. I'm not blaming you. But heck anyhow.

Gotta catch the bus. So long!

FLORA

P.S. Will you marry me? I'd love to have you.

Dear Charles,

It is with the greatest concern that I await an answer from you on November first, and lest you make, from insufficient knowledge, an irretrievable decision that will leave me long regretful, let me present what persuasion I can word in my own behalf.

Of all my best traits—tolerance, humor, adaptability—perhaps the most valuable in a chosen companion would be that of a strong zest for living, a desire to fill life with intensity, color and variety. I fear for many months after I met you this characteristic of mine was thoroughly but temporarily subordinated by unexplainable circumstances; but I have recovered it as the polar-star of my existence; and hope to live again with imagination, to design living with a view to orderly and graceful backgrounds of white fire-places and silver-edged mirrors; socially with teas by candlelight, culturally with recordings of *Jewels of the Madonna* and translations of Villon, practically with good waffles, and emotionally with a warm understanding of the needs of companionship.

My inheritance is an unbrokenly American one since 1723. I will fall heir to the ancestral house (nothing to brag about) and to the . . . stock (not a bad legacy). I have sufficient income for my needs, aside from food and shelter. I have no interfering or dependent relatives, have contracted no debts and have a genius for living well without money. My education includes one college, two universities and a business school; a little French, much music and no art; much Latin and no Greek. I have traveled up and down the Atlantic coast (U.S.) and thus enjoyed the broadening influence of varied contacts, and appeased youth's craving for single-handed adventure. Though well and kindly gaurded I have thus made valuable acquaintances from my father's law-associates in New York through Charleston's renegade socialites to Florida's politicians.

I love children and dogs and have been instructed by friends in the proper training of both. I have good health and no objections to perpetuating the species. I wish to make C. my home, so have interested myself in many of its activities, joined its Country Club; been careful, though therefore slow, to choose friends. I swim excellently, ride horseback well, dance nicely, play bridge indifferently and read aloud abominably. I no longer desire to become the despair of the Saints Above and I can follow the Episcopal service without a prayer book.

Most notably, I am reasonable, keep my word and arrive at conclusions without the necessity of argument. On the basis of affection, admiration and common interests I should find marrying you a delightful pact for mutual benefit. Should it, as a contract, prove otherwise, I assure you I would be entirely tractable and undemanding; if a mistake emotionally speaking, I assure you—"that I can go like snow and leave no trace behind."

ALICE

[Passport Photo]

Proposition: That the herein portrayed person be considered as follows:
Name: Hans Coldbrook
Age: 22
Description: Brown hair, grey eyes, 185 pounds, 6 ft. tall, healthy
Occupation: Philosopher of sorts, poet, relief worker, naturalist.
Aims: To demonstrate by living that Love equals life.
To build a home that will be the hub of a beloved community.
To stock it with healthy, lustful, intelligent children.
Experience: None of an immediate pertinent sort.
Desire: To be about the business of life with thy loving comradeship.

Please find enclosed self-addressed stamped envelope for reply.

WESTERN UNION (06)

MAY 25 1939
JOHANNA HENRY BENNINGTON VERMONT

NOT HARVEST TIME YET BUT WILL YOU TAKE ME ANYWAY STOP FUN IN THE HAY ISNT THE HALF OF IT ALL LOVE * JIM

New York, February 29, 1940

Dear Dick,

This being the last day of Leap Year, I had better get my proposal in.

Darling, will you marry me?

Your own
GLORIA

Americana

THE DISCOVERY of a new world and of the simple life as a religious experience is mirrored in the proposals of the early colonists in America.

Colonial houses saw short widowhoods; widowers remarried as quickly as they could get mates. The scarcity of women allowed these to pick and choose, in log cabins as well as in plantation mansions.

The diaries of pious men are delicious proof of how eagerly they obeyed the Lord (who did not mean them to "lead a widower's life") and their own amorous impulses.

Girls often took the lead—like clever Betsy Hanford of Virginia. The Reverend John Call who had baptized her was asked by one of her suitors to use his influence to impress upon her the Christian duty of marrying. The Reverend talked to Betsy and did his best to make her accept the unsuccessful suitor. She accepted the principle but not the object. Pressed for reasons she told the minister he would find the motive for her refusal in the Bible. She asked him to look up II Samuel

XII:7. Returning to his study he turned to the chapter and verse and saw these words:
"Thou art the man."
A few months later a notice in the *Virginia Gazette* announced the marriage of the Reverend Call to Betsy Hanford.

Roger Williams, pioneer of religious liberty (admired by the poet John Milton for leaving Europe and "finding a safe refuge for the sacred arc of conscience" in America) wanted to marry Jane Whalley, a relation of Sir William Masham, whose chaplain he was at the time. He wrote to Jane's aunt, Lady Barrington, with whom the girl was staying, in Spring 1629:

To his honourable good Ladie Ye Lady Barrington
                                      at Hatfield Priorie
Madam,
    Many and often speeches have long fluttered and floune abroad concerning your Laddiship's neere kinswoman and my unworthy selfe ... I presume therefore to consult with yr Laddiship, especially considering her loving and strong affection together with ye report as story abroad. The neerness of her blood to yr Laddiship and godly flourishing branches hath forc't me to confess her Portion, in yt regard, to be beyond compare invaluable ... Yet many feares have much possest me, Longe I have to discover yt sinceritie and Godliness which makes ye Lord himself to like his Creature and must make me if ever I have receued some good Testimonials from my own experience more from others not the least from your good Laddiship selfe. Objections have come in about her spirits, much accused for passionate and hastie, rash and inconsistant, other feares

about her present condition it being some Indecorum for her to condescend to my low ebb there I somewhat stick; but were all this cleared, there is one barr not likely to be broken, and that is the present Estate of us both.

[Follow explanations of his financial position, after which he proceeds:]

I haue been told to open to yr Laddiship the whole Anatomie of this business. To wrong yiur precious name and answer her kind love with want would be like gall to all the honey of my life and marr my marriage joy . . . I shall add that for the present I know none in the world I more affect and (should the Lord say amen to those other regards) should doubtless have answered (if not exceeded) her affection.

Roger Williams to Lady Barrington
 Nineteen months later he sailed for the English colonies with a wife—but not Jane Whalley. Driven out of Boston for religious differences with John Winthrop and the Puritans, who also had come to the new world to seek religious tolerance, Roger Williams founded the city of Providence, Rhode Island, in 1636.

John Winthrop, first governor of Massachusetts, married at the age of seventeen Mary Forth, a wealthy woman five years his senior. She died in June 1615, leaving him six children. Winthrop then married Thomasine Clopton, who died in childbirth one year later. The persistent John then approached Margret Tyndall (cca March 1618)

To my dearest friend and most heartily beloved Mistress Margret Tyndal.

Havinge seariously considered of that unequal conflict wch for my sake thou didst lately sustaine, & sherein yet (although the odds were great) God beinge on they side thou gatest the victorye, I have had from hence a large provocation to acknowledge God's providence and special favour towards me, & to give him thankes for so great experience as hathe been offered me hereby of thy godliness, love, wisdom & inviolable constancie; wch as in itself it deserves all approbation, so in me it is of such vertue as the more I thinke of it the more it drawes and knitts me heart unto thee, and hathe settled that estimation of thy love therein, as (I am truely persuaded) nothinge but death shall abolishe and diminishe it. Such an invincible resolution could not have been founde in a poor fraile woman, had not thine armes been strengthened by the mighty God of Jacob. He it was wch gave another spirit to thyselfe & that good lady thy mother, wth Caleb & Josuah, constantly to followe the Lord against all discouragements of the greater parte, — yea when my selfe, too cowardly and unkindly ioined armes wth thine opposers against thee; But now doe I knwe thou lovest me, & hereby we may both be fully assured that this thing cometh of the Lorde.

Therefor it is my desire to confirme thy heart in this resolution; not that I fear any change (farre be suche a thought from me) but for that I wish thee a large addition of comfort to thy constancie, wch may molifie & heale up the scarres of suche wounds as may yet remaine of thy late conflicte. And now I will take libtie to deale freely wth thee since there is no need of persuasion, nor any feare of suspition of flaterye; & let me tell thee that as thou hast doone worthyly & Christianly, so thou hast doone no otherwise than became thee being one professinge to feare God & beleeve in him: for (what so ever I am or may be, yet) beinge, in thy accompt, a servant of God & one that thou mightst well hope to be furthered to heaven by (Amen I saye), & being offred unto thee by God, & thy selfe beinge as warrantably called to embrace the opportunitye as a woman might be, I see not how thou couldst have had peace to thine owne heart if thou hadst refused it; but thou mightest iustly have feared least, for wthdrawinge thy heart from God & leaninge to thine owne reason, he should have given thee over to some suche matche as should have proved a plague to thy soule all thy dayes. . . .

Mrs. Margret Tyndal and John Winthrop were married in April, 1618. Perhaps it is not irrelevant to add that Winthrop had an annual income of 700 pounds, a huge sum in those days. Before her death in 1647, Margret bore John Winthrop eight children, bringing the total output for Winthrop's three wives up to fifteen.

To prove that the previous letter is not merely an isolated case in the history of letter-writing, but that Winthrop could write another one like it at any time, we cite from the next letter he wrote to Margret Tyndal:

To my best beloved Mrs Margaret Tyndall
        at Great Maplested, Essex.
Grace, Mercie & peace, &c:

My onely beloved Spouse, my most sweet freind, & faithfull companion of my pilgrimage, the happye & hopefull supplie (next Christ Jesus) of my greatest losses, I wishe thee a most plentifull increase of all true comfort in the love of Christ, wth a large & prosperous addition of whatsoever happynesse the sweet estate of holy wedlocke, in the kindest societye of a lovinge husbande, may afforde thee. Beinge filled wth the ioye of thy love, & wantinge opportunitye of more familiar communion wth thee, wch my heart fervently desires, I am constrained to ease the burthen of my minde by this poore helpe of my scriblinge penne, beinge sufficiently assured

that, although my presence is that wch thou desirest, yet in the want thereof, these lines shall not be unfruitfull of comforte unto thee. And now, my sweet love, lett me a whyle solace my selfe in the remembrance of our love, of wch this springe tyme of or acquaintance can putt forthe as yet no more but the leaves & blossomes, whilest the fruit lyes wrapped up in the tender budde of hope. . . .

John's father, Adam Winthrop, wrote to his future daughter-in-law in a warmer and more attractive way:

I am, I assure you, Gentle Mistress Margret, alredy inflamed with a fatherly affection towarde you; but nowe throughe the manifest tokens of your true love, and constant minde, whch I perceyve to be setteled in you towards my sonne, the same is exceedingly increased in mee. So that I cannot abstaine from expressinge it unto you by my pen in absence wch my tongue and mouthe I hope I shall shortly declare unto you in presence. And then I doubte not I shall have just cause to prayse God for you to thincke my selfe happy that in my old age I shall injoye the familiar company of so virtuous and loving a daughter, and passe the residue of my daies in peace and quietness. For I have hitherto had greate cause to magnifie his holy name for his loving kindness and mercy shewed unto me and my children and in those to whom they have been married; that both I have alwayes dearly loved and affected them, and they also most lovinglye and dutyfullye have used me. And therefore I assure you, Good Mistress Margret, That whatsoever love and kindness you shall vouchsafe to shewe hereafter unto mee, I will not only requite it with the like, but also to the utter most of my power redouble the same. And for that I woulde fayne make it a little parte of your faythe to beleeve, that you shall be happy in matching with my sonne,

I do here faithfully promise for him (in the presence of the almighty God) that he will alwaies be a most kind ande loving husbande unto you and a provident stewarde for you and yours during his life, and also after his deathe. Thus with my hearty recommendacions to your selfe, and to the Good lady your deere Mother, confirming my true Love and promise by a token of smale value, but of pure substance which I send you by this trusty bearer, I do leave you to the protection of the most mighty Trinitye.

This last day of March 1618
        Your assured frende
                ADAM WINTHROP

Forth Winthrop to his father, asking permission to propose to Ursula Sherman

Most louinge Father,

I would be loath soe far to violate the laws of nature or infringe the praecepts of nurture, and education, as to undertake any enterprize of moment without your leaue, knowledge, consent and license: that therefore I may haue your councell, and direction I desire that from me you may understand, that I doe beare affection in such sort as God may approue, and with your agreement may in time blesse with his holy ordinance of Marriage to my cosen Ursula, my aunt Fones her daughter, yet haue I med noe mention of any such thing, nor till I shall know your will, pleasur and advice herein will I. To your wisdom therefore doe I most humblye submitte myselfe, and earnestly desiring your prayers, that God may direct me for the best, I shall awaite the expecattion of your councell, instruction and direction, what best you in your wisdome shall see most fittinge for me to be done or left undone, and soe committing this to you and you to the protection of the allmighty with my most humble duty remembered to your selfe, my uncle an my aunt Downing, with my love to my cosens I rest and remaine

                your obedient sonne

From Groton Nouem: 17   FORTH WINTHROP
    1629

This match did not materialize, for a year later Forth had died.

The Reverend Dr. Cotton Mather had lost his wife December the first, 1702. In February 1703 he records in his diary:

There is a young Gentlewoman of incomparable Accomplishments. No Gentlewoman in the English America has had a more polite Education. She is one of rare Wit and Sensed of a comely Aspect; and extremely Winning in her Conversation, and she has a Mother of an extraordinary Charachter for her piety.

This young Gentlewoman first addresses me with diverse letters and then makes me a Visit at my House; wherein she gives me to understand, that she has long had a more than ordinary Value for my Ministry; and that since my present Condition has given her more of Liberty to think of me, she must confess herself charmed with my Person, to such a degree that she could not but break in upon me, with her most importunat Requests that I should make her mine; and that the highest consideration she had in it was her eternal salvation, for if she were mine, she could not but hope the Effect of it would be, that she should also be Christ's.

I endeavored faithfully to sett before her all the discouraging circumstances attending me, that I could think of. She told me that she had weighed all those Discouragements, but was fortified and resolved with a strong Faith in the mighty God, for to encounter them all . . .

I was in a great Strait, how to treat so polite a

Gentlewoman, thus applying herself to me. I plainly told her that I feared whether her Froposal would not meet with unsurmountable oppositions from those who had great interest in disposing of me. . . .

In the mean Time, if I could not make her my own, I should be glad of being any way instrumental to make her the Lord's.

I turned my Discourse and my Design into that Channel; and with as exquisite Artifice as I could use I made my Essayes to engage her young Soul into Piety.

She is not much more than twenty years old. I know she has been a very aiery Person. Her Reputation has been under some Disadvantage.

What Snares may be laying for me I know not. Much Prayer with Fasting and Patience must be my way to encounter them.

Dr. Cotton Mather fights the 'Tenderness in his heart' for the gentlewoman who has thus besieged him; but when a rumour gets round that he is engaged to her it turns out that her reputation is worse than he thought, and he chooses a Gentlewoman within two houses of his own, of unspotted reputation.

On 14 d. 5m (July) Wednesday, give my first Visit unto that lovely Gentlewoman. I was entertained with more than ordinary Civility, Affection and Veneration. And I found her to be an abundantly more agreable Person, than ever I imagined. (Her name is Mrs. Elisabeth Hubbard. She was married and quickly left a widow four year ago, and is now thirty Years of Age.) I see she will be a great gift of Heaven unto me, and astonishing reparation of my Loss, and Compensation for all the Grief I have mett withal. If I may live to see her illuminating my family, I shall reap a rich harvest of the Tears, the Fasts and the Resignations, with which I have been so long in addressing Heaven, under the deplorable Circumstances, of about fifteen Months together.

July 17, 1703

The Rage of that young Gentlewoman whom out of obedience to God I have rejected, (and never more pleased God than in rejecting of her addresses to me) is transporting her; to threaten that she will be a Thorn in my Side, and contrive all possible Wayes to vex me, affront me, disgrace me, in my Attempting a Return to the Married State with another Gentlewoman . . .

My Conversation with the lovely Person, to whom Heaven has directed me, goes on, with pure, chast, noble Strokes, and the Smiles of God upon it.

And the Universal Satisfaction which it has given to the People of God, thro Town and Country, proclames itself ,to a Degree which perfectly amazes me.

August 18, 1703

This is the Day, the joyful Day, wherein my glorious Lord Jesus Christ brings me to the rich Harvest of my Prayers and Tears . . . I am in the Evening of this Day, to receive a most lovely Creature and such a Gift of Heaven unto me, and mine, that the Sense thereof almost as often as I ponder theron, dissolves me into Tears of Joy.

I resolved that I would spend the Day in Heaven, if the Lord would please to open unto me His Heaven. I spent the whole Day in my Study, devoting it as a solemn Thanksgiving to the Lord. . . .

In The Evening, my Father married me, unto a Wife, in finding of whom, I have to my Astonishment found Favour of the Lord. . . .

On August 24. Tuesday. I brought my lovely Consort home; and made an agreeable Entertainment at my House, for the Relatives of both.

Samuel Sewall, colonist, minister, judge in the Salem witch case, was one of those full-blooded Puritans who loved life, enjoyed good food and knew how to drive a bargain. He married three times, always putting the responsibility on the Lord. His famous diary describes his courtships after the death of his first wife, Judith Hull, who had borne him thirteen children. The widow Winthrop advises him to buy a new wig. Mrs. Denison tells him to procure another and better nurse. Whereupon he writes into his diary: "My bowels yearn towards the widow Denison; but I think God directs me in his providens to desist." The widow Tilly is willing; he marries her at the age of sixty-five, but she falls sick on the wedding-night and leaves him a widower again after half a year. Still undaunted in spirit he writes, at seventy, to the Widow Gibbs and is accepted. They were married in March, 1722.

February 6, 1718. This morning wondering in my mind whether to live a single or a married life. I had a sweet and very affectionate meditation concerning the Lord Jesus. Nothing was to be objected against his Person, Parentage, Relations, Estate, House, Home! Why did I not resolutely, presently, close with Him! And I cry'd mightily to God that He would help me so to doe!

March 14. Deacon Marion comes to me, sits with me a great while in the evening; after a great deal of discourse about his courtship . . . He told me the Olivers said they wish'd I would court their aunt. I said little, but said 'twas not five months since I buried my dear wife. Had said before 'twas hard to know whether best to marry again or no. Whom to marry. Gave him a book of the Berlin Jewish Converts.

March 19. Mr. Leverett, when he and I are alone, told me his wife and he had laid out Madam Brown for me, and yet took occasion to say that Madam Winthrop had done very generously by the Major General's (her former husband's) family in giving up her dower. I said if Madam Brown should leave her fair accommodations at Salem, she might be apt to repent it.

April 7. I prove Mr. William Denison's will. Her brother Edmund brought the widow to town, and gave me notice beforehand. Mr. Door took occasion in her absence to say she was one of the most dutifull wives in the world. Her cousin, the widow Hayden, accidentally came with her.

June 9. Mrs. Denison came in the morning about 9 o'clock, and I took her up into my Chamber and discoursed thorowly with her; told her I intended to visit her at her own house next Lecture-day. She said 't would be talked of. I answered in such cases persons must run the gantlet....

June 17. Went to Roxbury Lecture, visited Governor Dudley and Mrs. Denison, gave her Dr. Mather's sermons very well bound. Told her we were in it invited to a wedding. She gave me very good curds....

July 17. My son from Brooklin being here, I took his horse and visited Mrs. Denison. I told her 'twas time now to finish our business. Ask'd her what I should allow her. She not speaking. I told her I was willing to give her two hundred and fifty pounds per annum during her life if it should please God to take me out of the world before her. She answered she had better keep as she was, than give a certainty for an uncertainty. She should pay dear for coming to dwell at Boston. I desired her to make proposals, but she made none. I had thought of publishment next Thursday the sixth. But I now seem to be far from it. May God, who has the pity of a father, direct and help me!

July 28. Having consulted with Mr. Walter after Lecture, he advised me to goe and speak with Mrs. Denison. I went this day in the Coach, and had a fire made in the Chamber where I spake with her before on July 1. I enquired how she had done these three or four weeks. Afterwards I told her our conversation had been such when I was with her last, that it seem'd to be a direction in Providence, not to proceed any further. She said, It must be what I pleased, or to that purpose. . . . But she said it was hard to part with all property and have nothing to bestow on her kindred. I said I did not intend anything of the movables. . . . She asked me if I would drink. I told her yes. She gave me cider, apples and a glass of wine. Gathered together the little things I had given her and offered them to me, but I would take none of them. Told her I wish'd her well, should be glad to hear of her welfare. She seem'd to say she should not again take in hand a thing of this nature. Thanked me for what I had given her and desired my prayers. . . . Got home about nine at night. Laus Deo. My bowels yearn towards Mrs. Denison, but I think God directs me in his providence to desist.

* * *

August 29, 1719. I visit Mrs. Tilly the second time. It seems she was born in Elisabeth's town in the Jerseys. In her 20th year when she married Mr. Woodmansey.

September 2. Visit Mrs. Tilly and speak with

her in her Chamber. Ask her to come and dwell at my house. She expresses her unworthiness of such a thing with much respect. I tell her of my going to Bristol. I would have her consider of marrying. She answered she would have me consider of it.

September 16. After the Meeting I visited Mrs. Tilly.

September 18. ditto.

September 21. I gave Mrs. Tilly a little book entitled "Ornaments for the Daughters of Zion." I gave it to my dear wife August 28, 1702.

September 24. Eat almonds and reasons with Mrs. Tilly and Mrs. Armitage. Discoursed with Mrs. Armitage, who spake very agreably, and said Mrs. Tilly had been a great blessing to them, and hoped God would make her to me and my family.

Oct. 26 or 27. I visited Dr. Increase Mather, designing to ask him to marry me. I ask'd him whether it was convenient to marry on the evening after the Thanksgiving. He made me no answer. I ask'd agen. He said Mr. Prince had been with him to marry him; he told him he could not go abroad in the evening. Then I thought twas in vain to proceed any further; for Mrs. Tilley's preparations were such that I could not defer it any longer; and could not be married sooner, because I was out-published on the Thanksgiving day and not before.

Oct. 29. Thanksgiving-day: between 6 and 7, Brother Moodey and I went to Mrs. Tilley's' and about 7, or 8, were married by Mr. J. Sewall, in the best room below stairs. Mr. Prince pray'd the 2nd time. Mr. Adams the Minister of Newington was there. Mr. Oliver and Mr. Timothy Clark, Justices, and many more. Sung the 12th, 13th, 14th, 15th, and 16th verses of the 90th Psalm. Cousin S. Sewall set Low-Dutch Tune in a very good Key, which made the singing with a good number of voices very agreeable. Distributed cake. Mrs. Armitage introduced me into my Brides Chamber after she was a-bed. I thank'd her that she had left her room in that Chamber to make way for me, and pray'd God to provide for her a better lodging, so none saw us after I went to bed. Quickly after our being a-bed my bride grew so very bad she was fain to sit up in her bed; I rose to get her Petit Coats about her. I was excedingly amaz'd, fearing lest she should have dy'd. Through the favour of God she recover'd in some considerable time of her fit of the tissick, spitting partly blood. She herself was under great consternation.

Friday, Oct. 30. Governor Shute, Governor Dudley and his Lady, Councillors and Ministers in town with their wives dined with us.

May 26, 1720. Went to bed after ten. About eleven or before my dear wife was opressed with a rising of flegm that obstructed her breathing. I arose and lighted a candle, made Scipio give me a bason of water. About midnight my dear wife expired to our great astonishment, especially mine.

* * * *

September 5, 1720. Going to Son Sewall's I there meet with Madam Winthrop, told her I was glad to meet her there, had not seen her for a great while; gave her Mr. Homes's Sermon.

September 30. Went to Mr. Colman's Lecture. Daughter Sewall acquaints Madam Winthrop that if she pleas'd to be within at 3 P. M. I would wait on her. She answer'd she would be at home.

Oct. 1 . . . . Satterday, I dine at Mr. Stoddard's: from thence I went to Madam Winthrop's just at 3. Spake to her, saying, my loving wife died so soon and suddenly, 'twas hardly convenient for me to think of Marrying again; however, I came to this Resolution that I would not make any Court to any person without first Consulting with her. Had a pleasant Discourse about 7 (seven). Single persons sitting in the Fore-seat viz. Madm Rebekah Dudley, Catharine Winthrop, Bridget Usher, Deliverance Legg, Rebekah Loyd, Lydia Colman, Elizabeth Bellingham. She propounded one and another for me; but none would do, said Mrs. Loyd was about her age.

Oct. 6 . . . A little after 6 p. m. I went to Madam Winthrop's She was not within. I gave Sarah Chickering, the Maid 2s, Juno., who brought in wood, 1s. Afterward the Nurse came in, I gave her 18d, having no other small Bill. After awhile Dr. Noyes came in with his Mother [Madam Winthrop —ed.] and quickly after his wife came in: They sat talking, I think, till eight a-clock. I said I feared I might be some Interruption to their Business; Dr. Noyes reply'd pleasantly: He feared they might be an Interruption to me, and went away. Madam seem'd to harp upon the same string. Must take care of her Children; could not leave that House and Neighbourhood where she had dwelt so long. I told her she might doe her children as much or more good by bestowing what she laid out in Housekeeping, upon them. Said her Son would be of Age the 7th of August. I said it might be inconvenient for her to dwell with her Daughter-in-Law, who must be Mistress of the House. I gave her a piece of Mr. Belcher's Cake and Ginger-Bread wrapped up in a clean sheet of Paper; told her of her Father's kindness to me when Treasurer, and I Constable. . . .

Oct. 11th. I writ a few Lines to Madam Winthrop to this purpose: "Madam, These wait on you with Mr. Mayhew's Sermon, and Account of the State of the Indians on Martha's Vinyard. I thank you for your unmerited favours of yesterday; and hope to have the Hapiness of Waiting on you tomorrow before Eight a-clock after Noon. I pray GOD to keep you, and give you a joyfull entrance upon the Two Hundred and twenty ninth year of Christopher Columbus his Discovery; and take Leave, who am, Madam, your humble Servt.

S. S.

Oct. 17. In the evening I visited Madam Winthrop, who Treated me Courteously, but not in clean linen as sometimes. She said she did not know whether I would come again or no. I ask'd her how she could so impute inconstancy to me. Gave her this day's Gazett.

Oct. 19. Midweek, Visited Madam Winthrop; Sarah told me she was at Mr. Walley's, would not come home till late. Was ready to go home: but said if I knew she was there I would go thither. Sarah seem'd to speak with pretty good Courage, She would be there. I went and found her there, with Mr. Walley and his wife in the little Room below. At 7 a-clock I mentioned going home; at 8 I put on my Coat, and quickly waited on her home. She found occasion to speak loud to the servant, as if she had a mind to be known. Was Courteous to me; but took occasion to speak pretty earnestly about my keeping a Coach: I said 'twould cost 100 pounds per anum: she said 'twould cost but 40 pounds.

Oct. 21. Friday, My Son, the Minister, came to me P.M. by appointment and we pray one for another in the old Chamber; more especially respecting my Courtship. About 6, a-clock I go to Madam Winthrop's! Sarah told me her Mistress was gone out, but did not tell me whither she went. She presently order'd me a Fire; so I went in, having Dr. Sibb's Bowels with me to read. A while after I heard Madam Winthrop's voice, enquiring something about John. After a good while and Claping the Garden door twice or thrice, she came in. She received me Courteously. I ask'd when our proceedings should be made publick: She said They were like to be no more publick than they were already. Offer'd me no wine that I remember. I rose up at 11 a'clock to come away, saying I would put on my Coat. She offer'd not to help me. I pray'd her that Juno might light me home, she open'd the Shutter, and said twas pretty light abroad; Juno was weary and gon to bed. So I came home by Starlight as well as I could.

Octobr 24. I went in the Hackny Coach through the Comon, stop'd at Madam Winthrop's. I told her, I was come to enquire whether she could find it in her heart to leave that House and Neighbourhood, and go and dwell with me at the South-End. I think she said softly, Not Yet. I told her It did not lay in my Lands to keep a Coach. If I should I should be in danger to be brought to keep Company with her Neighbour Brooker, (he was a little before sent to prison for Debt) .... As to a Perriwig, my best and greatest Freind, I could not possibly have a greater, began to find me with Hair before I was born, and had continued to do so ever since; and I could not find in my heart to go to another. She commended the book I gave her, Dr. Preston, the Church Marriage; quoted him saying 'twas inconvenient keeping out of a Fashion commonly used. I said the Time and Tide did circumscribe my visit. She gave me a Dram of Black-Cherry Brandy, and gave me a lump of the Sugar that was in it. ...

Novr 4th. Friday, Went again about 7 a-clock; found there Mr. John Walley and his wife: sat discoursing pleasantly; I shewed them Isaac Moses's (an, Indian) writing. Madam W. serv'd Comfeits to us. After a-while a Table was spread, and supper was set. I urg'd Mr. Walley to Crave a Blessing; but he put it upon me. About 9 they went away. I ask'd Madam what fashioned Neck-lace I should present her with. She said, None at all. I ask'd her Whereabout we left off last time; mention'd what I had offer'd to give her; Ask'd her what she would give me; She said she could not Change her Condition: She had said so from the beginning; Could not be so far from her Children, and the Lecture. Quoted the Apostle Paul affirming that a single life was better than a Married . . . .

Monday, November 7th . . . . I went to Mad. Winthrop: found her rocking her little Katee in the cradle. I excus'd my coming so late (near Eight). She set me an armed Chair and Cusheon; and so the Cradle was between her armed chair and mine. Gave her the remnant of my Almonds; She did not eat of them as before; but laid them away; I said I came to enquire whether she had altered her mind since Friday, or remained of the same mind still. She said, Thereabouts. I told her I loved her and was so fond as to think that she loved me: She said she had a great respect for me . . . . She gave me a Glass of Wine. I think I repeated again that I would go home and bewail my Rashness in making more haste than good Speed. I would endeavor to contain myself, and not go on to Sollicit her to do that she could not Cnsent to. Took leave of her. As I came down the steps she bid me have a Care. Treated me Courteously . . . I did not bid her draw off her glove as sometime I had done. Her dress was not so clean as sometime it had been. Jehovah Jireh!

Nov. 11. Went not to Mme Winthrop. This is the second Withdraw.

Satterday, July 15, 1721 . . . . Call and sit awhile with Madam Ruggles . . . . I shewed my willingness to renew my old acquaintance; she expressed her inability to be Serviceable. Gave me cider to drink. I came home.

Thursday, August 3rd. Went in the Coach and visited Madam Ruggles after Lecture. She seems resolved not to move out of that house. Maybe of some use there — none at Boston — till she be carried out; made some Difficulty to accept the Election Sermon, lest it should be an obligation on her. . . . .

Samuel Sewall to the Widow Gibbs
Jan^v 12th $1721-22$

Madam,

Your Removal out of Town, and the Severity of the Winter, are the reason of my making you this Epistolary Visit. In times past (as I remember) you were minded that I should marry you, by giving you to your desirable Bridegroom. Some sense of this intended Respect abides with me still; and puts me upon enquiring whether you be willing that I should Marry you now, by becoming your Husband; Aged, and feeble, and exhausted as I am, your favourable Answer to this Enquiry, in a few Lines, the Candor of it will much oblige, Madam, your humble $Serv^t$

S.S.

Madam Gibbs.

This is the shortest proposal letter written before the twentieth century. It got results; S. P. was accepted.

Samuel Parr to Jane Morsingale   Undated

Madam, You are a very charming woman, and I should be happy to obtain you as a wife. If you accept my proposal I will tell you who was the author of Junius.

This is typical of the colonial proposals. They were nearly always directed to the parent; the children had not much say in the matter. They were, as a seventeenth century manual on the "Duty of Man" held it, so much the property of their parents, that to give themselves away without consent would have been called theft.

To Mr. Jeremiah Moore   *176—?*
Dear Sir,

My son, Mr. John Walker, having informed me of his intention to pay his addresses to your daughter Elizabeth, if he should be agreable to yourself, lady and daughter, it may not be amiss to inform you what I feel myself able to afford for their support, in case of a union. My affairs are in an uncertain state, but I will promise one thousand pounds, to be paid in 1766, and the further sum of two thousands pounds I promised to give him; but the uncertainty of my present affairs prevents my fixing on a time of a payment. The above sums are all to be in money or lands and other effects at the option of my son, John Walker.

                                                             THOMAS WALKER

Abraham Lincoln, as a young clerk in a Salem store, had fallen in love with Anne Rutledge, the daughter of his landlord. When she died of malaria, a nervous depression clouded his life.

He then moved to Springfield and formed a new attachment. The object was Mary Owens, "bouncing, sensible lass." The letter of proposal written to her is highly unusual. She turned him down.

Two years later he found himself engaged to Mary Todd, a beautiful girl of high spirits and higher social origin than he. The wedding day was set, everything prepared, the guests waiting; but he either forgot to turn up in church or failed in some other blatant way. A scandal flared up which was never quite explained. The engagement was broken off in January, 1841, but there was a reconciliation a year later and they were married in November, 1842.

Abraham Lincoln to Mary Owens

Springfield, Illinois, May 7, 1837.

Friend Mary:

I have commenced two letters to send you before this, both of which displeased me before I got half done and so I tore them up. The first I thought was not serious enough, and the second was on the other extreme. I shall send this, turn out as it may.

This thing of living in Springfield is rather a dull business, after all; at least it is so to me. I am quite as lonesome here as I ever was anywhere in my life. I have been spoken to by but one woman since I have been here, and should not have been by her if she could have avoided it. I've never been to church yet, and probably shall not be soon. I stay away because I am conscious I should not know how to behave myself.

I am often thinking of what we said about your coming to live at Springfield. I am afraid you would not be satisfied. There is a great deal of flourishing about in carriages here, which it would be your doom to see without sharing it. You would have to be poor, without the means of hiding your poverty. Do you believe you could bear that patiently? Whatever woman may cast her lot with mine, should any ever do so, it is my intention to do all in my power to make her happy and contented; and there is nothing I can imagine that would make me more unhappy than to fail in the effort. I know I should be much happier with you than the way I am, provided I saw no signs of discontent in you. What you have said to me may have been in the way of jest, or I may have misunderstood it. If so, then let it be forgotten; if otherwise, I much wish you would think seriously before you decide. What I have said I will most positively abide by. My opinion is that you had better not do it. You have not been accustomed to hardship, and it may be more severe than you now imagine. I know you are capable of thinking correctly on any subject, and if you deliberate maturely upon this before you decide, then I am willing to abide by your decision.

You must write ma a good long letter after you get this. You have nothing else to do, and though it might not seem interesting to you after you have written it, it would be a good deal of company to me in this "busy wilderness". Tell your sister I don't want to hear any more about selling out and moving. That gives me the "hypo" whenever I think of it.
      Yours etc.
                LINCOLN

August 16, 1837

Miss Mary S. Owens:

Friend Mary: You will no doubt think it rather strange that I should write you a letter on the same day on which we parted, and I can only account for it by supposing that seeing you lately makes me think of you more than usual; while at our late meeting we had but few expressions of thought. You must know that I cannot see you or think of you with entire indifference; and yet it may be that you are mistaken in regard to what my real feelings toward you are. If I knew you were not, I should not trouble you with this letter. Perhaps any other man would know enough without further information; but I consider it my peculiar right to plead ignorance, and your bounden duty to allow the plea. I want in all cases to do right, and most particularly so in all cases with women. I want at this particular time, more than anything else, to do right with you; and if I knew it would be doing right, as I rather suspect it would, to let you alone, I would do it. And for the purpose of making the matter as plain as possible, I now say that you can now drop the subject, dismiss your thoughts (if you had any) from me forever, and leave this letter unanswered, without calling forth one accusing murmur from me. And I will even go further, and say that if it will add anything to your comfort or peace of mind to do so, it is my sincere wish that you should. Do not understand by this that I wish to cut your aquaintance. I mean no such thing. What I do wish is that our further aquaintance shall depend upon yourself. If such further aquaintance would contribute nothing to your happiness, I am sure it would not to mine. If you feel yourself in any degree bound to me, I am now willing to release you, provided you wish it; while, on the other hand, I am willing and even anxious to bind you faster, if I can be convinced that it will, in any considerable degree, add to your happiness. This, indeed, is the whole question with me. Nothing would make me more miserable than to believe you miserable — nothing more happy than to know you were so.

In what I have now said I believe I cannot be misunderstood, and to make myself understood is the whole object of this letter.

If it suits you best to not answer this, farewell. A long life and a merry one attend you. But if you conclude to write back, speak as plainly as I do. There can be neither harm nor danger in saying to me anything you think, just in the manner you think it.

My respects to your sister.
                Your friend,
                            LINCOLN.

Mrs. Bennett Able, Mary's sister, was anxious for the match to come off, but Mary found the suitor 'deficient in the little links that make up a woman's happiness.' When a party went out riding and other men helped their ladies at a bad crossing, Lincoln would ride ahead and not even look back to see how she was getting across; and when they were climbing a steep hill and she was carrying her sister's fat baby, he didn't offer to help her carry. Besides, he said 'Ain't' instead of 'isn't' and 'sich' instead of 'such'— and Mary had been trained in Kentucky schools for refined young ladies.

The rejected suitor got the whole affair out of his system by writing this description of it to his friend Mrs. O. H. Browning:
Abraham Lincoln to Mrs. O. H. Browning:
Describing a proposal to a lady not named.

Springfield, 1 April 1838.
Dear Madam:
Without apologizing for being egotistical, I shall make the history of so much of my life as has elapsed since I saw you the subject of this letter. And, by the way, I now discover that in order to give a full and intelligible account of the things I have done and suffered since I saw you, I shall necessarily have to relate some that happened before.

It was, then, in the autumn of 1836 that a married lady of my acquaintance, and who was a great friend of mine, being about to pay a visit to her father and other relatives residing in Kentucky, proposed to me that on her return she would bring a sister of hers with her on condition that I would engage to become her brother-in-law with all convenient despatch. I, of course, accepted the proposal, for you know I could not have done otherwise had I really been averse to it; but privately, between you and me, I was most confoundedly well pleased with the project. I had seen the said sister some three years before, thought her intelligent and agreeable, and saw no good objection to plodding life through hand in hand with her. Time passed on, the lady took her journey, and in due time returned, sister in company, sure enough. This astonished me a little, for it appeared to me that her coming so readily showed that she was a trifle too willing, but on reflection it occurred to me that she might have been prevailed on by her married sister to come, without anything concerning me ever having been mentioned to her, and so I concluded that if no other objection presented itself, I would consent to waive this. All this occurred to me on hearing of her arrival in the neighborhood—for, be it remembered, I had not yet seen her, except about three years previous, as above mentioned. In a few days we had an interview, and, although I had seen her before, she did not look as my imagination had pictured her. I knew she was over-size, but she now appeared a fair match for Falstaff. I knew she was called an "old maid", and I felt no doubt of the truth of at least half of the appellation, but now, when I beheld her, I could not for my life avoid thinking of my mother; and this, not from withered features, — for her skin was too full of fat to permit of its contraction into wrinkles, — but from her want of teeth, weather-beaten appearance in general, and from a kind of notion that ran in my head that nothing could have commenced at the size of infancy and reached her present bulk in less than thirty-five or forty years; and, in short, I was not at all pleased with her. But what could I do? I had told her sister that I would take her for better or for worse, and I made a point of honor and conscience in all things to stick to my word, especially if others had been induced to act on it, which in this case I had no doubt they had, for I was now fairly convinced that no other man on earth would have her, and hence the conclusion that they were bent on holding me to my bargain. "Well", thought I, "I have said it, and, be the consequences what they may, it shall not be my fault if I fail to do it." At once I determined to consider her my wife, and this done, all my powers of discovery were put to work in search of perfections in her which might be fairly set off against her defects. I tried to imagine her handsome, which, but for her unfortunate corpulency, was actually true. Exclusive of this, no woman that I have ever seen has a finer face. I also tried to convince myself that the mind was much more to be valued than the person, and in this she was not inferior, as I could discover, to any with whom I had been acquainted.

Shortly after this, without attempting to come to any positive understanding with her, I set out for Vandalia, when and where you first saw me. During my stay there I had letters from her which did not change my opinion of either her intellect or intention, but, on the contrary, confirmed it in both.

All this while, although I was fixed "firm as the surge-repelling rock" in my resolution, I found I was continually repenting the rashness which had led me to make it. Through life I have been in no bondage, either real or imaginary, from the thraldom of which I so much desired to be free. After my return home I saw nothing to change my opinion of her in any particular. She was the same, and so was I. I now spent my time in planning how I might get along in life after my contemplated change of circumstances should have taken place, and how I might procrastinate the evil day for a time, which I really dreaded as much, perhaps more, than an Irishman does the halter.

After all my sufferings upon this deeply interesting subject, here I am, wholly, unexpectedly, completely out of "the scrape", and I now want to know if you can guess how I got out of it—out, clear, in every sense of the term — no violation of word, honor, or conscience. I don't believe you can guess, and so I might as well tell you at once. As the lawyer says, it was done in the manner following, to wit: After I had delayed the matter as long as I thought I could in honor do (which, by the way, had brought me round into the last fall), I concluded I might as well bring it to a consummation without further delay, and so I mustered my resolution and made the proposal to her direct; but, shocking to relate, she answered, No. At first I supposed she did it through an affectation of modesty, which I thought but ill became her under the peculiar circumstances of her case, but on my renewal of the charge I found she repelled it with greater firmness than before. I tried it again and again but with the same success, or rather with the same want of success.

I finally was forced to give it up, at which I very unexpectedly found myself mortified almost beyond endurance. I was mortified, it seemed to me, in a hundred different ways. My vanity was deeply wounded by the reflection that I had so long been too stupid to discover her intentions, and at the same time never doubting that I understood them perfectly and also that she, whom I had taught myself to believe nobody else would have, had actually rejected me with all my fancied greatness. And, to cap the whole, I then for the first time began to suspect that I was really a little in love with her. But let it all go! I'll try and outlive it. Others have been made fools of by the girls, but this can never with truth be said of me. I most emphatically, in this instance, made a fool of myself. I have now come to the conclusion never again to think of marrying, and for this reason — I can never be satisfied with any one who would be blockhead enough to have me.

When you receive this, write me a long yarn about something to amuse me. Give my respects to Mr. Browning.

A. L.

General George E. Pickett, born in Richmond, Virginia, in 1825, fought at Gettysburg under Robert Lee; his charge of the ridge, though he set out with five thousand men and came back with less than fifteen hundred, is counted among the great heroic deeds of the time.

Two letters of proposal he wrote to La Salle Corbell, who was engaged to him—they were more than proposals, in fact: urgent appeals to come into camp and marry him. They had met when she was a little child, visiting her grandmother during an epidemic of whooping-cough. The little girl was unhappy in her isolation—she could not join in the games, the merry dancing and singing of other children, and pressed her little nose against the window-panes of houses watching the merry-making inside. Her little heart was near breaking when one morning, playing alone at the beach, she saw an officer lying on the sand, under the shelter of an umbrella—"I had noticed him several times, always apart from the others, and very sad. I could imagine but one reason for his desolation, and in pity for him I crept under his umbrella to ask him if he too had the whooping-cough. He smiled and answered, no; but as I still persisted he drew me to him, telling me that he had lost someone who was dear to him. He was very lonely—and straightway, without so much as a by your leave, I promised to take the place of his dear one, and comfort him in his loss...I crept from under the umbrella pledged to Lieut. George E. Pickett, U.S.A., for life and death. I still hold most sacred a little ring and a locket he gave me on that day. I have always called him 'my soldier.'"

The following letter, written on the eve of the battle, is here reprinted with permission of Houghton, Mifflin and Co. from their book "Soldier of the South" edited by Arthur Crew Inman and published in 1928.

General Pickett to La Salle Corbell

In Camp, April 15, 1863

This morning I awakened from a beautiful dream, and while its glory still overshadows the waking and fills my soul with radiance, I write to make an earnest request—entreating, praying, that you will grant it. You know, my sweetheart, we have no prophets in these days to tell us how near or how far is the end of this awful struggle. If the battle is not to the strong, then we may win; but when all our ports are closed and the world is against us, when for us a man killed is a man lost, while Grant may have twenty-five of every nation to replace one of his, it seems that the battle is to the strong. So often already has hope been dashed to the winds....

Now, my Sallie, may angels guide my pen and help me to write—help me to voice this longing desire of my heart and to intercede with you for me for a speedy fulfilment of your promise to be my wife. As you know, it is imperative that I should remain at my post and absolutely impossible for me to come for you. So you will have to come to me. Will you, dear? Will you come? Can't your beautiful eyes see beyond the mist of my eagerness and anxiety that in the bewilderment of my worship—worshipping, as I do, one so divinely right, and feeling that my love is returned, how hard it is for me to ask you to overlook old time

heart responded to the call, what could I do but adhere to the social laws more formidable than cannons? My soldier admitted that I was right and we agreed to await a more favorable time.

General George E. Pickett to La Salle Corbell

Culpepper, July 23, 1863

You will perceive my own darling Sallie that we are again on this side of the Blue Ridge. The campaign in Maryland and Pennsylvania was short and terrible. Would that we had never crossed the Potomac, or that the splendid army which we had on our arrival in Pennsylvania had not been fought in detail. If the charge made by my gallant Virginians on the fatal third of July had been supported, or even if my other two brigades had been with me, I would now, I believe, have been in Washington and the war ended. But alas, dearest, God has willed it otherwise, and I fear there will be many more blood-drenched fields and broken hearts before the end does come....

For three days and nights I have been almost constantly in the saddle. Last night the 22 I had a tent pitched and sat down to a meal at a camp table, the first time since leaving Bunker Hill. We had been going al fresco—when we did sleep it was with the heavens for a canopy and a fence rail for a pillow. We shall be here three or four days, perhaps longer.

I thank the great and good God that he has spared me to come back and claim your promise, and I pray your womanly assistance in helping me to its *immediate* fulfill-

customs, remembering only that you are to be a soldier's wife? A week, a day, an hour, as your husband, would engulf in its great joy all my past woes and ameliorate all future fears.

So, my precious one, don't delay; send me a line back by Jackerie saying you will come. Come at once, my own, into this valley of the shadow of uncertainty, and make certain the comfort that if I should fall I should fall as your husband.... Think, my dear little one, of the uncertainty and dangers of even a day of separation, and don't let the time come when either of us will look back and say, "It might have been."

If I am spared, my precious, all my life shall be devoted to making you happy, to keep all that might hurt you far from you, to making all that is good come near you. Heaven will help me to be ever helpful to you, and will bless me to bless you. If you knew how every hour I kneel at your altar, you would know how much your answer will mean to me, and how, while I plead, I am held back by a reverence and a sensitive adoration for you. For, Sallie, you are my goddess, and I am only

Your devoted,
SOLDIER

Note by Sallie attached to the above letter.

To those who recall the rigid system of social training in which a girl of that period was reared, it will not seem strange that a maiden, even in wartime, could not seriously contemplate leaving home and being married by the wayside in that desultory and unstudied fashion. So, though my

ment. This is no time for ceremonies. The future is all too uncertain, and it is impossible for me to call a moment my own. Again, with all the graves I have left behind me, and with the wretchedness and misery this ill-fated campaign has caused, we would not wish anything but a silent and very quiet wedding.

I gave Colonel Harrison a good-luck piece (parting gift to me of the officers of the Pacific) and told him to have it made into a wedding ring, engraved G. E. P. and S. C. Married———and to leave sufficient space for date and motto which you would direct.

Your
Soldier

This appeal no "rigid system" could resist. Sallie came and they were married.